A JETER PRESS PAMPHLET
ENGAGING IDEAS *at the* CROSSROADS OF
FAITH *and* FREEDOM

O AMERICA!

—————————

A MANIFESTO *on* LIBERTY

DERRICK G. JETER

JETER PRESS

McKinney, Texas

2011

—♦♦♦♦※♦♦♦♦—

SUCH PAPERS *cannot* FAIL *to* PRODUCE *the* BEST EFFECT.
THEY INFORM *the* THINKING PART *of the* NATION . . .
[*and*] SET *the* PEOPLE *to* RIGHTS.[1]

THOMAS JEFFERSON *to* JAMES CALLENDER
on the IMPORTANCE *of* PAMPHLETS
OCTOBER 6, 1799

—♦♦♦♦※♦♦♦♦—

—◦◦◦※◦◦◦—

The
DEDICATION

FOR CHRISTINA
and THOSE WHO GIVE THEIR LIVES *to*
SECURE *the* BLESSINGS *of* LIBERTY

—◦◦◦※◦◦◦—

TABLE *of* CONTENTS

—⁓⁓※⁓⁓—

O AMERICA,

THY GOD *did* EXPECT BETTER THINGS

from THEE *and* THY CHILDREN.[2]

WILLIAM STOUGHTON

—⁓⁓※⁓⁓—

O AMERICA!

—⁍—

A MANIFESTO *on* LIBERTY

LIBERTY IS RARELY LOST THROUGH REVOLUTION — the sudden, violent upheaval of arms. Liberty is usually lost through devolution — the slow, imperceptible erosion of the animating principles of freedom. Every generation must guard against such erosion by shoring up those principles — or risk losing liberty altogether. Without vigilance and courage, a day may come when this generation awakens to find the America we know and love has become a mere memory of days long ago. In its place will lie the reality of a liberty-less land.

America's founding generation understood the delicacy of liberty. They understood that inattention and cowardice to guard liberty could shatter it. As Justice Louis Brandeis said, our Founders "believed liberty to be the secret of happiness and courage to be the secret of liberty."[3] The founding generation possessed courage in excess. They demonstrated their courage when they heeded the warning of George Whitefield, the revivalist minister from Great Britain: "My heart bleeds for America. . . . There is a deep laid plot against both your civil and religious liberties, and they will be lost. Your golden days are at an end. You have nothing but trouble before you."[4] When trouble came a decade later that generation met it with pluck and warded off the fate Whitefield predicted.

Like the Founding Fathers, Ronald Reagan also knew how easily America might lose her liberty. And like Whitefield, Reagan also pronounced a sobering truth, advising his and future generations of liberty's perilous existence:

> Freedom is never more than one generation away from extinction—we didn't pass it to our children in their bloodstream. It must be fought for, protected, and handed on for them to do the same, or one day we will spend our sunset years telling our children and our children's children what it was like in the United States when men were free.[5]

The question for us is simple: will we meet the challenge of fighting for, protecting, and passing on liberty with the same courage and wisdom as our forefathers?

To answer this question, we must first understand the state of liberty in twenty-first century America. We must also understand how we arrived at this state and what we must do to secure and maintain liberty for ourselves and our posterity.

THE STATE *of* LIBERTY TODAY

IF WE TAKE AN HONEST LOOK AT FREEDOM, we must conclude that in many important ways we are more free than were our fathers and mothers of the founding generation. This is especially true for African Americans, Native Americans, and women. Yet, in significant ways we are less free than those who founded the United States.

Advances in technology, large-scale corporate fraud, and the ever-present threat of terrorism have put us all under the ever-watchful eye of government. And for more than a half-century, government entitlements have reduced many of our fellow citizens to wards of the state. At every turn, government bureaucracy, at all levels, demands more from each individual and business. We pay the bills in dollars and red tape; but, the real cost is paid in liberty. We are no longer masters over our public servants; we are now servants under our public masters—a fact our forefathers would find distressing and indefensible.

But our decline in liberty did not occur in a mere generation or two. Rather, the slow erosion of individual freedom began in the early 1900s with the rise of the Progressive Era and its insistence on interpreting the Constitution, not according to the originators' intent but according to our ever-changing culture. As Progressives saw it, the Constitution must flex and bend with society's twists and turns. No longer should the nation adapt to a fixed point in the political sky. The polar star must move with the turning of national circumstances. Or, as was popular in the language of the time, the Constitution must evolve. Constitutional scholar Ronald Pestritto and historian William Atto observed:

> The Progressive Era was the first major period in American political development to feature, as a primary characteristic, the open and direct criticism of the Constitution. While criticism of the Constitution could be found during any period

of American history, the Progressive Era was unique in that such criticism formed the backbone of the entire movement. . . . [Progressives] knew that the limits placed on the national government by the Constitution represented major obstacles to implementing the progressive policy agenda. Progressives had in mind a variety of legislative programs aimed at regulating significant portions of the American economy and society and at redistributing private property in the name of social justice. The Constitution, if interpreted and applied faithfully, stood in the way of this agenda.[6]

The Founders wrote the Constitution in permanent ink, but in the hands of Progressives the ink began to fade.

Theodore Roosevelt, considered the first Progressive president, reshaped our understanding of the presidency, transforming it into a more energetic and dominant power among the intended constitutional equals of the legislative and judicial branches. Roosevelt's presidency is now the model for the modern presidency, regardless of party.

It was Woodrow Wilson, however, who significantly smudged the line between liberty and tyranny. In his 1913 book, *The New Freedom*, Wilson compared the Founders' writing and understanding of the Constitution to mechanical science—a completely wrongheaded view in Wilson's opinion.

> [The Founders] constructed a government as they would have constructed an orrery [a mechanical model of the solar system],—to display the laws of nature. Politics in their thought was a variety of mechanics. The Constitution was founded on the law of gravitation. The government was to exist and move by virtue of the efficacy of "checks and balances."
>
> The trouble with the theory is that government is not a machine, but a living thing. It falls, not under the theory of the universe, but under the theory of organic life. It is accountable to Darwin, not to Newton. It is modified by its environment, necessitated by its tasks, shaped to its functions by the sheer pressure of life. No living thing can have its organs offset against each other as checks and live. . . . Living political constitutions must be Darwinian in structure and in practice. Society is a

living organism and must obey the laws of life, not of mechanics; it must develop.

> All that progressives ask or desire is permission—in an era when "development," "evolution," is the scientific word—to interpret the Constitution according to the Darwinian principle; all they ask is recognition of the fact that a nation is a living thing and not a machine.[7]

Of course, insistence on a Darwinian interpretation of the Constitution means that those in power can interpret and apply the Constitution any way they choose: evolving meaning for evolving times. In contrast to the philosophy of Abraham Lincoln's "right makes might," legal evolutionists adhere to the philosophy of "might makes right"—that the possessors of power determine what is and what is not correct for the citizens of the country. And it is this philosophy that has held sway for the better part of a century. The Wilsonian/Darwinian model continues to dominate constitutional education, interpretation, and application, rallying judges, politicians, law professors, and law students under the banner: "The Constitution—A Living, Breathing Document."

Wilson's presidential acolytes include Franklin Roosevelt and his New Deal, Lyndon Johnson and his Great Society, and Barack Obama and his campaign to "fundamentally transform" America. President Obama, like Progressive presidents before him, has sided on increased constriction of liberty by gorging the government on the people's wealth. The attitude of "what's yours is mine" was alien to Americans and American presidents prior to the Progressive Era. Yet, this attitude today has resulted in ballooning deficits and debts into the tens of trillions of dollars and increased taxation and regulation. Lean years are ahead, not only for this generation of Americans but for generations to come. The requirements to kneel before a nameless and faceless bureaucracy, and foot the bill for its bulging budgets is a clear and present danger to individual liberty. The freedom to do with your wealth as you wish, the freedom to leave your property to your heirs without penalty, and the freedom to conduct business without cascading red tape are quaint ideas from a bygone era.

Liberty and bloated bureaucracy cannot dine at the same table. One produces, the other consumes. One creates, the other squanders. One made America the envy of the world, the other is making America just another country in the world. And yet, President Obama continues to fatten the federal government, the bureaucracy by feeding it a diet rich in taxes, deficits, and debts. And he does this under the cover of the Constitution. By interpreting the Constitution according to Wilson's method, the hand of government continues to pick the people's pantry clean.

Of particular importance to President Obama is the legislative trifecta of the sweeping overhaul of healthcare, the passage of comprehensive immigration reform, and the mushrooming of exhaustive environmental regulations. Since his election in 2008, ballooning deficits and debts have overshadowed this agenda, but if Obama is successful in persuading the Congress to pass such legislation, the risks and rewards of freedom will surrender to the phantom "security" of the state. American exceptionalism will give way to statism, making us little different than a European-style Socialist nation which seeks to secure the well-being of every citizen, legal and illegal, from womb to tomb . . . for a price.

But statism—the principle upholding the supremacy of the state over the supremacy of God and His gift of liberty to mankind—is antithetical to our American republic, to the very Founders who created and handed down our American republic. The Founders envisioned liberty for themselves and their posterity. They risked their lives, their fortunes, and their honor to achieve that liberty. And they established the Constitution to protect that liberty. It is liberty that should be the great aim of our government, as Thomas Jefferson wrote: "[The policy of the American government] is to leave their citizens free, neither restraining nor aiding them in their products."[8]

Yet, Jefferson was not naïve. He knew that liberty tends to retreat while government tends to advance. "The natural progress of things is for liberty to yield and government to gain ground," he observed.[9]

And so, it is true.

Our precipitous fall from freedom has been in the making for a century or more. The point has been long in coming, but it is now clear: we hold our liberty too cheaply. Too readily have we sold our liberty for the shackles of an ever-intrusive and inflated government. The question now is, *what, if anything, can we do to recover our former glory as the land of the free?*

Part of the answer lies in the remembrance that this is also the home of the brave. And bravery, as it was in our Founders' day, is the necessary requirement.

DIMINISHING *the* BLESSINGS OF LIBERTY

OUR FOUNDING FATHERS, when it came to securing, establishing, and maintaining a republic of liberty, believed in three fundamental principles—what we might call *the liberty triangle*: a republic cannot survive without liberty, liberty cannot survive without virtue, and virtue cannot survive without religion. Historian James Hutson called this "the founding generation's syllogism, which occurs repeatedly in every form of discourse from 1776 onward; virtue and morality are necessary; religion is, therefore, necessary for republican government."[10]

In 1772, four years before he signed the Declaration of Independence, Samuel Adams wrote that Americans had a religious obligation to stand against tyranny and for liberty.

> Is it not High Time for the People of this Country explicitly to declare, whether they will be Freemen or Slaves? It is an important Question which ought to be decided. It concerns us more than any Thing in this Life. The Salvation of our Souls is interested in the Event: For wherever Tyranny is establish'd, Immorality of every Kind comes in like a Torrent. It is in the interest of Tyrants to reduce

the people to Ignorance and Vice. For they cannot live in any Country where Virtue and Knowledge prevail. The Religion and public Liberty of a People are intimately connected; their Interests are interwoven, they cannot subsist separately; and therefore they rise and fall together. For this Reason, it is always observable, that those who are combined to destroy the People's Liberties, practice every Art to poison their Morals. How greatly then does it concern us, at all Events, to put a Stop to the Progress of Tyranny.[11]

In the Founders' view, no Declaration, no Constitution, and no law meant to pronounce, establish, or secure the people's liberty could withstand the ravages of religious and moral decay among the people. They believed that an assault on the people's liberty was a fools' pursuit, as long as the people governed themselves under the watchful eye of God and His Holy Scripture. So deeply rooted in the American character was this belief that Frenchman Alexis de Tocqueville upon visiting the United States in 1830 — fifty-four years after America declared her independence — observed:

Freedom sees in religion the companion of its struggles and its triumphs, the cradle of its infancy, the divine source of its rights. It considers religion as the safeguard of mores; and mores as the guarantee of laws and the pledge of its own duration.[12]

Yet, if ever the people allow their moral and religious convictions to grow shabby and soft, they will grow indifferent and cowardly toward their liberties, and their liberties will succumb to the plundering of an unprincipled and power-hungry government.

The truth of this downward spiral is repeated time and again throughout history. Within a century of their glorious emancipation from Egyptian slavery, the ancient Israelites fell into a predictable pattern of liberty and tyranny that lasted almost three hundred years. Each cycle began with shortsightedness—forgetting their history and the God who delivered them from bondage. Their forgetfulness led to sin, especially the sin of idolatry. Sin led to servitude, as one oppressor after another—Moabites, Canaanites, Midianites, Ammonites, or Philistines—enslaved the Hebrews. Shackles wrung from their hearts a cry of supplication for a deliverer. God answered their prayers and brought salvation through a Judge, who threw off the chains of slavery. Once free, silence fell upon the land and the Israelites lived in peace . . . until a new generation grew shortsighted. And the cycle began again.

This cycle was broken with the coronation of King Saul. But liberty under the reign of a king is more limited than liberty under the reign of God. This was the message of God's prophet. But the people demanded a king. God instructed Samuel, the last Judge in Israel, to "'Listen to the voice of the people in regard to all that they say to you, for they have not rejected you, but they have rejected Me from being king over them'" (1 Samuel 8:7). Nevertheless, God told Samuel to warn the people about life under a king:

> "This will be the procedure of the king who will reign over you: he will take your sons and place them for himself in his chariots and among his horsemen and they will run before his chariots. He will appoint for himself commanders of thousands and of fifties, and some to do his plowing and to reap his harvest and to make his weapons of war and equipment for his chariots. He will also take your daughters for perfumers and cooks and

bakers. He will take the best of your fields and your vineyards and your olive groves and give them to his servants. He will take a tenth of your seed and of your vineyards and give to his officers and to his servants. He will also take your male servants and your female servants and your best young men and your donkeys and use them for his work. He will take a tenth of your flocks, and you yourselves will become his servants. Then you will cry out in that day because of your king whom you have chosen for yourselves, but the Lord will not answer you in that day." (1 Samuel 8:11–18)

The people refused to listen to Samuel, and they cried out all the more: "No, but there shall be a king over us, that we also may be like all the nations, that our king may judge us and go out before us and fight our battles" (8:19–20).

The people got their king, and he did exactly as Samuel predicted. In the course of time, the kingdom of Israel would divide into north and south. In 722 BC the godless Northern Kingdom of Israel was destroyed by the Assyrian Empire. In 605 BC the Babylonian king Nebuchadnezzar marched through the Southern Kingdom of Judah and took captives. Nebuchadnezzar returned in 597 BC in response to a rebellion, and finally destroyed Judah, along with God's temple in Jerusalem, in 586 BC.

The Israelites did not taste the fruits of freedom for another 2,500 years—from that day in 586 BC, when Nebuchadnezzar destroyed Jerusalem, until AD 1948 when the modern nation-state of Israel was founded. And all because their religious and moral convictions grew shabby and soft, making them indifferent to their liberties— liberties ripe for the picking by unprincipled and power-hungry kings and kingdoms.

The ancient Israelites, however, are hardly alone in their example of how a people might lose their liberties. Look to the ancient Greeks and Romans who followed a similar pattern of decline: religion gone to seed, growing immorality, historic amnesia, consuming selfishness, and deepening dependence on the public dole. Gone were the virtues which made those empires great: faith, courage, self-reliance, selflessness, memory, community, and self-control.

The ravages of history wiped those empires from the map. Thus far, America has escaped such historical deletion. But if we are to remain a free country, we must remain a free people—a people of faith and virtue capable of governing ourselves. If not, then all that is left to us are the accidents of history, as Robert Bork noted in *Slouching Towards Gomorrah*:

> Men were kept from rootless hedonism, which is the end state of unconfined individualism, by religion, morality, and law. These are commonly cited. To them I would add the necessity for hard work, usually physical work, and the fear of want. These constraints were progressively undermined by rising affluence. The rage for liberty [personal license and the removal all constraints imposed by religion and virtue] surfaced violently in the 1960s, but it was ready to break out much earlier and was suppressed only by the accidents of history. It would be possible to make a case that conditions were ripe at the end of the nineteenth century and the beginning of the twentieth but that the trend was delayed by the Great War [World War I]. The breaking down of restrictions resumed in the Roaring Twenties. But that decade was followed by the Great Depression, which produced a culture whose behavior was remarkably moral and

law-abiding. The years of World War II created a sense of national unity far different from the cultural fragmentation of today. The generations that lived through those times of hardship and discipline were not susceptible to extreme hedonism, but they raised a generation that was.

Affluence reappeared in the late 1940s and in the decade of the 1950s and has remained with us since. . . . Affluence brings with it boredom. Of itself, it offers little but the ability to consume, and a life centered on consumption will appear, and be, devoid of meaning. Persons so afflicted will seek sensation as a palliative, and that today's culture offers in abundance.[13]

History's lesson is stark but unmistakable: when citizens abandon God, private virtue fails; when private virtue fails, public virtue fails; and when public virtue fails, society fails, requiring either the passage of more laws or the machinations of history to govern a people no longer capable of governing themselves.

Cultural observer and scholar Michael Novak put it this way: "[The United States] ought to have, when it is healthy and when it is working as it is intended to work, [300] million policemen—called *conscience*. When there are [300] million consciences on guard, it is surprising how few police are needed on the streets."[14] A society which esteems virtue is a society which governs itself. A society which scorns virtue can't hire enough policemen to govern those who won't govern themselves. It's quite simple really: greater self-government means fewer laws and greater liberty; less self-government means greater laws and less liberty. It is either self-rule under the auspices of virtue and religion, or increased and increasing government intrusion, or the mercies of history. What else is there?

America is at a crossroads. Will we return to the ideas of our Founders, who believed in limited government and near unlimited liberty, or will we continue down the path laid out by Progressives, who favor near unlimited government and limited liberty? The choice is ours to make. If we hope to turn around without further injury to our freedom, we must first face this truth: we have been too forgetful for too long.

FORGETTING GOD

The ancient book of Deuteronomy called the Israelites back to remembrance—to remember how God delivered them from Egypt and sustained them in the wilderness. They were to remember so as to not fall prey to the culture in which they were entering. For if they forgot their God, they would worship idols and thereby receive judgment, instead of blessing, from the living God.

America is not Israel. But God loves and blesses those nations that honor Him. Says the psalmist: "Blessed is the nation whose God is the LORD" (Psalm 33:12). And though we celebrate the First Amendment's protection that all are free to worship God according to conscience, America has long held to the creed of "In God We Trust." We sing "God Bless America" and pledge our allegiance to "one nation under God." But have these sentiments lost their meaning in the hearts and minds of Americans; have they become bland upon our tongues? What if America were to forget God's many blessings? What if our citizens were to forget that God rules in the heavens and will judge the living and the dead? What if we were to forget God altogether?

The great Russian novelist and social critic Aleksandr Solzhenitsyn, upon receiving the 1983 prize from the Templeton Foundation, made this startling admission:

> If I were asked today to formulate as concisely as possible the main cause of the ruinous [Russian] Revolution that swallowed up some sixty million of our people, I could not put it more accurately than . . . "Men have forgotten God; that's why all this has happened." . . . And if I were called upon to identify briefly the principle trait of the entire twentieth century, here too I would be unable to find anything more precise and pithy than to repeat once again: "Men have forgotten God."[15]

We may, as others have, dismiss Solzhenitsyn as a crank crying in a foreign wilderness, but one of our own, an American president known for his perceptive and penetrating mind, came to the same conclusion in his day:

> Whereas it is the duty of nations as well as of men, to own their dependence upon the overruling power of God, to confess their sins and transgressions, in humble sorrow, yet with assured hope that genuine repentance will lead to mercy and pardon; and to

recognize the sublime truth, announced in the Holy Scriptures and proven by all history, that those nations only are blessed whose God is the Lord:

And, insomuch as we know that, by His divine law, nations like individuals are subjected to punishments and chastisements in this world, may we not justly fear that the awful calamity of civil war, which now desolates the land, may be but a punishment, inflicted upon us, for our presumptuous sins, to the needful end of our national reformation as a whole People? We have been preserved, these many years, in peace and prosperity. We have grown in numbers, wealth, and power, as no other nation has ever grown. But we have forgotten God. We have forgotten the gracious hand which preserved us in peace, and multiplied and enriched and strengthened us; and we have vainly imagined, in the deceitfulness of our hearts, that all these blessings were produced by some superior wisdom and virtue of our own. Intoxicated with unbroken success, we have become too self-sufficient to feel the necessity of redeeming and preserving grace, too proud to pray to the God that made us! [16]

What Abraham Lincoln and Aleksandr Solzhenitsyn understood was the truth that no nation founded upon religious principles can maintain its liberty once God is forgotten—consigned to the fringes of public life or cast out altogether. In all cases, the citizens of such countries exchange their liberty for tyranny. Russia fell under the bleak ideology of Soviet Communism. Germany fell under the jackbooted dictums of Nazi Fascism. And America in the 1860s fell under the bloody sword of civil war.

Thomas Jefferson's haunting questions, then, remain as relevant today as they were in the 1780s:

> Can the liberties of a nation be thought secure when we have removed their only firm basis, a conviction in the minds of the people that these liberties are of the gift of God? That they are not to be violated but with his wrath? Indeed I tremble for my country when I reflect that God is just: that his justice cannot sleep forever.[17]

The corrosive philosophies of secularization and privatization have eaten away at the once firmly held conviction that religion is the vital bulwark of liberty. Today, religious ideas are considered either pointless or poisonous to the health of the republic and, therefore, should be confined to the private and personal spheres only. We have bought the lie that the church must maintain a secondary and separate role in the life of our republic. God is an outlaw in our schools; children who pray in public are pariahs; the Ten Commandments are forbidden in public places; and Christmas celebrations are taboo.

Serious court challenges have been leveled against our once treasured mottos: "One nation under God," "In God We Trust," and "God Bless America." And we, the guardians of liberty—a liberty our Founders passed on to us—go about our lives with a callous indifference to the dismantling of our religious heritage. The blood of our Founders would run hot knowing that their sacrifices have wrought such godless notions and gutless concern among their posterity.

Is it any wonder that America has slowly slid toward despotism for more than a century now? In a very practical sense we have replaced "In God We Trust" with "In Government We Trust," believing that government programs like Social Security, welfare, and healthcare will transform America into a utopia—a perfect place that never was and never will be, a place where God is no longer needed. The fictional state of utopia mattered not to Progressives like Woodrow Wilson, Franklin Roosevelt, or Lyndon Johnson. And today, it little concerns Barack Obama. According to Progressives, a utopia—no matter how futile the pursuit or how high the cost in national treasure or individual liberty—is what we must strive to achieve.

There was a time when government was far away, but God was close at hand. Today, wherever God may be, the government has slipped its hand into ours. And for very many of our citizens, it is government, and not God, that is provider and sustainer. In this then, the state has taken the place of God—it is the new faith, the new creed, the new religion, just as Georg Hegel predicted in *Philosophy of History*: "The state is the divine idea as it exists on earth."[18] And in *Philosophy of Rights* Hegel wrote:

> The state is the march of God in the world; its ground or cause is the power of reason realizing itself as will. When thinking of the idea of the state, we must not have in our mind any particular state, or particular institution, but must rather contemplate the idea, this actual God, by itself. . . . We must hence honor the state as the divine on earth."[19]

All the state requires of its supplicants is the sacrifice of their freedom!

The United States hasn't yet reached the destination of such an idolatrous despotism; nevertheless, we have already started to stroll down that dark and dismal street by experimenting with European-style socialism. Whether it is progressive taxation of personal income and inheritance, or providing birth-to-death welfare, or bailouts and buyouts of private corporations (such as Citigroup, Goldman Sachs, and General Motors), or regulating student loans, or mandating universal healthcare, each government program shoos liberty and trust in a gracious God into the shadows and asks American citizens to place their lives into the hands of nameless and faceless bureaucrats. When what we should do is heed the warning of one who knew what it meant to live under the unlit tyranny of Communism as well as in the light of freedom. Solzhenitsyn declared:

> Within the philosophical system of Marx and Lenin, and at the heart of their psychology, hatred of God is the principle driving force, more fundamental than all their political and economic pretensions. Militant atheism is not merely

incidental or marginal to Communist policy; it is not a side effect, but the central pivot. To achieve its diabolical ends, Communism needs to control a population devoid of religious and national feeling, and this entails the destruction of faith and nationhood.[20]

Historically, purveyors of political power, even those devoid of God, knew the truth of what Tocqueville observed: "In America, it is religion that leads to enlightenment; it is the observance of divine laws that guides man to freedom."[21] So, all the government need do to control the people of the United States is make certain, in Tocqueville's words, "the destruction of faith and nationhood."[22] Faith and freedom—they are inextricably bound. So is soft-headed but hard-hearted atheism and socialism.

CORRUPTED VIRTUE

Samuel Adams advised that "neither the wisest constitution nor the wisest laws will secure the liberty and happiness of a people whose manners are universally corrupt."[23] He was echoing a similar sentiment spoken by his cousin, John Adams:

We have no government armed with power capable of contending with human passions unbridled by morality and religion. Avarice, ambition, revenge, or gallantry would break the strongest cords of our Constitution as a whale goes through a net. Our Constitution was made only for a moral and a religious people. It is wholly inadequate to the government of any other.[24]

It bears repeating: failure of private virtue produces failure in public virtue. This in turn gives birth to a growing government, which is compelled to control a people no longer capable of controlling themselves.

For example, in the wake of the 2008 financial meltdown, Congress passed new legislation to reform Wall Street, to curb Wall Street's greed. It was legislation that cost taxpayers hundreds of billions of dollars. But the greed of insurance companies, Wall Street investment and banking firms, and other large corporations which contributed to the financial crisis was not, as some claim, the fault of capitalism.

The invigorating spirit of capitalism is the free market, where opportunities are equal, even if outcomes are unequal. The practice of ethical capitalism, as understood by our Founding Fathers, always benefits the whole. Most of our ancestors believed in and heeded Paul's warning: "The love of money is a root of all sorts of evil" (1 Timothy 6:10). "Greed is not good," was our Founders' unspoken motto. But we have rejected our ancestors' wisdom and now shout with full throats: "Greed is good!" Greed has become our god—to the ruination of our liberty.

We've reached this blasphemous state because we have forgotten our morals—forgotten the virtues of frugality and simplicity. These virtues are not natural to man, though the vice of hungering for ever more is. The virtues which could have prevented the economic collapse are spiritually informed and come by way of submission to God. Of course, one can only submit if one remembers that God is in His heavens judging the intentions and actions of a selfish and sinful humanity.

Greed is capitalism corrupted and is immoral. On the other hand, overindulgent welfare is socialism and also is immoral. An old American axiom states: "You can't get something for nothing." This is true of government as well as business. Tocqueville expanded on this axiom in his landmark book, *Democracy in America*. He warned of benign appearing governments that give handouts with one hand while picking your pocket with the other. Governments may not pick your pocket of cash (though they might), but they *will* pick your pocket of liberty if too much charity is expected from bureaucracy.

Tocqueville wrote:

> An immense tutelary power is elevated, which alone takes charge of assuring [the citizens'] enjoyments and watching over their fate. It is absolute, detailed, regular, far-seeing, and mild. It would resemble paternal power if, like that, it had for its object to prepare men for manhood; but on the contrary, it seeks only to keep them fixed irrevocable in childhood. . . . So it is that every day it renders the employment of free will less useful and more rare; it confines the action of the will in a smaller space and little by little steals the very use of it from each citizen. Equality has prepared men for all these things: it has disposed them to tolerate them and often even to regard them as a benefit. Thus, after taking each individual by turns in its powerful hands and kneading him as it likes, the sovereign extends its arms over society as a whole . . . and finally reduces each nation to being

nothing more than a herd of timid and industrious animals of which the government is the shepherd.[25]

A government that provides social services for a people who could and should do for themselves has no interest in its citizens acting like adults but rather like children in perpetual childhood. Worse, such a government treats these "children" like cattle. But people are not cattle. People carry within them the image of God and are made to reflect His image. One of the surest ways human beings, whether rich or poor, reflect God's image is through work.

In Scripture, wealthy landowners were commanded by God not to harvest their entire fields but to leave the edges—the gleanings—unharvested for the poor, so the poor might thereby provide for their families (Leviticus 23:22). A beautiful picture of this is found in the book of Ruth (2:1–18). Why did God make such a provision? Because honest work, rewarded with honest pay, affirms a person's dignity; it declares that that individual is an image bearer.

As we'll explore later, not all welfare is immoral nor deprives its recipients of humanity. Yet, an all-protective state that divvies up welfare to those not in desperate need decreases the motivation to work and dehumanizes the poor. This has always been true, regardless of the people, the place, or the period of history. Edward Gibbon observed this fact while writing about the fall of the Roman Empire:

> The frequent and regular distributions of wine and oil, of corn or bread, of money or provisions, had almost exempted the poorer citizens of Rome from the necessity of labour. . . . It was artfully contrived by Augustus that, in the enjoyment of plenty, the Romans *should lose the memory of freedom*.[26]

Gibbon's description is often summarized as "bread and circuses"—full bellies and entertaining diversions lead not to freedom but to fetters.

Recipients of paternal welfare become dependent upon the state, losing the memory of independence and the dignity of work. They gradually find themselves treated by the state as no better than infantile adults or worse: cattle receiving a ration of food stamps and herded into dilapidated and dangerous housing projects. No! We *must* do better. We *can* do better. Men and women were not created for this; they were created to work—rich and poor alike. Men and women were created to bear God's image and represent Him on earth as creators. In fulfilling this high calling and noble responsibility we bear within our beings divine dignity—dignity that comes not from the hand of the state but from the hand of the Almighty.

Beyond dehumanizing the poor, undue welfare also compounds its immorality by setting up a system of envy and thievery. While the poor often covet the rich and their riches (leading to frustration and hatred) the government, often with well-meaning but misplaced compassion, engages in theft under the guise of legal taxation—taxes intended to distribute resources—convinced that the wealth of the rich belongs to the state.

The government, therefore, imposes higher and higher taxes on the wealthy to ensure that the rich pay their "fair share." The state, then, out of its deep well of "mercy" redistributes those monies to the poor in the form of handouts or government programs, perpetuating the degrading treatment of the poor as children or as cattle. This is a vicious, vile, and villainous cycle—a cycle without precedent in the history of America but readily found in the history of communist/socialist countries. Karl Marx and Friedrich Engels outlined a rough sketch of this cycle in their infamous manifesto:

The communist revolution is the most radical rupture with traditional property relations; no wonder that its development involves the most radical rupture with traditional ideas. . . .

The first step in the revolution by the working class is to raise the proletariate to the position of ruling class, to win the battle of democracy.

The proletariate will use its political supremacy to wrest, by degrees, all capital from the bourgeoisie, to centralize all instruments of production in the hands of the state, i.e., of the proletariate organized as the ruling class, and to increase the total of productive forces as rapidly as possible.[27]

Marx's and Engels's high sounding words about the rise of the working class notwithstanding, the proletariate in the old Soviet Union never did become the ruling class. The ruling class before the Russian Revolution of 1917 (the bourgeoisie) was simply replaced by another ruling class to whom the working class had to answer. The proletariate, however, didn't know (and couldn't have known) that at the time. They were persuaded that Marx's and Engles's promise of a benign, government-run communist utopia would usher in a new world order—one in which equality would rule. The equalizing of economic disparity would come about through the application of ten points, some of which are in practice—in whole or in part—in America today. The following are those points, numbered as they are in Marx's and Engles's *Communist Manifesto*:

2. A heavy progressive or graduated income tax.

3. Abolition of all right of inheritance.

5. Centralization of credit in the hands of the state, by means of a national bank with state capital and an exclusive monopoly.

6. Centralization of the means of communication and transport in the hands of the state.[28]

The clear intention of our country's Founders was equality of opportunity in a free society. The clear intention of those who champion an unthinking welfare system and the redistribution of wealth is radical egalitarianism— equality of outcome. This is not what the Founders intended.

Without a doubt, some taxes are needed for the maintenance of what our Founders envisioned as a small, limited constitutional government. Taxes collected in an effort to enrich the poor and win votes may prove effective for the politician at the ballot box but not so for the bank account of the poor. Such payments to the poor only keep them impoverished and beholding to an imperial despot who allows them to feed at the public trough. The poor will never become rich by demanding the rich become poor. To believe otherwise is both foolish and foul.

Many of the rich and the poor have fallen into the glut of greed. And many, alike, seek to accumulate wealth for their own selfish ends. But the government, as well, populated by supposed compassionate leaders and bureaucrats, is just as greedy—hungering for power to control the rich person's wealth and the poor person's poverty, thereby controlling their lives. Only an immoral and impious people would submit to such "compassion" instead of demanding real compassion—the compassion that teaches the moral lesson that "if a man will not work, then he will not eat" (2 Thessalonians 3:10).

It must be granted, of course, that some of our citizens are destitute and need real, immediate assistance.

Nevertheless, the government is the wrong vehicle to administer such help.

Governments are notoriously inefficient, expensive, and if left unchecked, corrupt. Local communities—neighbors, churches, and private organizations—should come to the rescue, helping these individuals and families get on their feet.

Perhaps the greatest story ever told was the one told by Jesus, the one of the good Samaritan (Luke 10:30–36). By using a despised man—the Samaritan—as the hero of the story, Jesus removed all barriers to the truth that love—practical, simple love—for another human being was a significant step in the fulfillment of God's law (10:27). James, the brother of Jesus, never forgot the lesson. With a masterstroke of his pen, James wrote: "Pure and undefiled religion in the sight of our God and Father is this: to visit orphans and widows in their distress" (James 1:27). For people of faith, the command is direct and challenging: be a neighbor to those in need; be a Samaritan; "Go and do likewise" (Luke 10:37).

If your immediate and focused compassion brings recovery to those in need within your community, they, through honest labor, may now truly reflect God's image by providing for themselves and their families, and thus contribute to the good of the community.

This is virtuous and right.

This is how it was intended.

This is liberty.

HISTORIC AMNESIA

Chuck Colson—who made history as Richard Nixon's hatchet man in the White House, who was a convicted felon in the Watergate debacle, and who went on to become one of the most influential voices in Christendom in the late twentieth and early twenty-first centuries—described in his Templeton Prize address what awaits those who are careless about history:

> Disdaining the past and its values, we flee the judgment of the dead. We tear down memory's monuments—removing every guidepost and landmark—and wander in unfamiliar country. But it is a sterile wasteland in which men and women are left with carefully furnished lives and utterly barren souls.[29]

History can hurt.

If you are a friend of history, you know how far we've fallen from what our Founders intended for their posterity and for the government charged with preserving the liberties of their posterity. And you know looking back on that path can be painful. But most Americans don't know history. Numerous studies have shown that high school and university students routinely fail basic tests covering American history and civics. Vigen Guroian, a respected professor at The University of Virginia, made this troubling observation:

> Those who are in special positions of influence within a society, whether they are parents or politicians, clergy, teachers, or press, are obligated to exercise that society's collective memory to ensure that its tradition of freedom is handed on and renewed. Yet as a college professor I can say confidently and with great sadness that the young men and women in my classroom are the most historically illiterate and politically uninformed that I have seen in more than twenty-five years of teaching. The fault does not rest solely on their teachers. It rests at least as much on parents,

pastors, and civic leaders. All have allowed the rising generation to become captive to a popular culture that is self-centered, hedonistic, dangerously utilitarian, increasingly antagonistic to memory, and impious toward the past.[30]

As quoted in the introduction of this pamphlet, Reagan stated that the love of liberty does not pass to our children through our DNA. We only light liberty's torch for other generations by loving America's history and taking the time to demonstrate that love in the presence of our children, teaching them the importance of knowing and honoring the past.

In the movie *Amistad*, Anthony Hopkins portrayed John Quincy Adams. Standing before the Supreme Court, arguing for the freedom of a band of Africans, Hopkins's Adams closed with a reference to history's memory. Walking past the busts of the Founding Fathers, Adams identified each man:

James Madison, Alexander Hamilton, Benjamin Franklin, Thomas Jefferson, George Washington, John Adams . . . we have long resisted asking you for guidance. . . . [But] we understand now, that we've been made to understand, and to embrace the understanding, that who we are is who we were. We desperately need your strength and wisdom, to triumph over our fears, our prejudices, ourselves.[31]

John Quincy Adams was right, the wasteland we find ourselves in today is a direct result of our failure to understand the wisdom of history, to ask history for guidance, and to remember our founding principles — principles that maintain that God is the giver of rights, that our rights are inalienable, and that governments are instituted among men to secure our rights. These same principles assert that when the government becomes tyrannical and seeks to invalidate our rights, we have the duty to redress our government and, if necessary, rebel.

When it came time to form a new government, our Founders wisely articulated our American values in the Preamble of the Constitution, beginning with the source of political power:

We the People of the United States, in order to form a more perfect union, establish justice, insure domestic tranquility, provide for the common defense, promote the general welfare, and secure the blessings of liberty to ourselves and our posterity (emphasis mine).

Most of us today would still give an amen to these powerful words. Unfortunately, they're the only governing words many of us know.

If we don't bother to read the Declaration of Independence, the Constitution, and the Bill of Rights and wrestle with the ideas therein, how can we know if our rights are being (or have been) trampled under foot by government? The answer is obvious: we can't.

Could it be that our amnesia of American history and our ignorance of America's founding documents are the reasons why our liberty and that of our posterity is a mere shadow of what it was when our forefathers professed our freedoms in the Declaration of Independence? Their covenant was wholehearted: "And for the support of this Declaration, with a firm reliance on the protection of divine Providence, we mutually pledge our lives, our fortunes, and our sacred honor." Was their vow in vain? Liberty is imperiled when the people cannot detect lies; and the people cannot detect lies when they forget, never learn, or refuse to learn their history.

The greatest danger to us lies not without but within. The surest way to destroy a country is to destroy its liberty . . . from the inside. And once inside, the surest way to destroy a country's liberty is to destroy its memory—its history.

Regarding the maintenance of our liberty, our Founders hung their hopes on a religious and virtuous citizenry who would govern themselves under the watchful eye of God in obedience to His Scripture and in accordance with our historic documents. From among this religious and virtuous group of individuals, our Founders envisioned honorable leaders emerging whom the citizenry could trust to govern them. These historically informed and virtuously motivated elected representatives were expected to govern their communities, their states, and their nation in the same manner they governed themselves—with wisdom, piety, frugality, integrity, courage, and a strict adherence to the rule of law as prescribed in our written Constitution. Only with the fulfillment of this vision would our republic of liberty be free from peril.

Tragically, on the whole, this has not been the case in America's more recent history.

SECURING *the* BLESSINGS OF LIBERTY

FOR FAR TOO LONG our legislators, presidents, and judges have failed to live up to the high calling the American people have entrusted to them. But all is not lost. Our situation is not hopeless.

Better things can be expected and achieved.

We must never forget that our republic will only endure in freedom for as long as God wills. Yet, as American citizens, we must exert every effort to preserve and protect the blessings of liberty, keeping ever on our lips the humble prayer of patriotism: *God, may our country last forever in freedom.*

"The genius of the United States," Walt Whitman wrote, "is not best or most in its executives or legislatures, nor in its ambassadors or authors or colleges or churches or parlors, nor even in its newspapers or inventors . . . but always most in the common people."[32] If we are to reclaim our country and re-form it into the nation of which our Founders dreamt, then we must become the people our republic requires—people of faith and noble character, who hold the nation's memories dear.

The way forward is the way back. To live up to the expectations of our Founders, we must commit ourselves anew to three goals: one spiritual, one moral, and one intellectual.

A SPIRITUAL GOAL: REMEMBER GOD

"Where the Spirit of the Lord is, there is liberty" (2 Corinthians 3:17). If we mean to hold on to the liberty which we have for so long enjoyed, then we must return to God. Tocqueville was correct when he wrote:

> Despotism can do without faith, but freedom cannot. Religion is much more necessary in [a] republic . . . and in democratic republics more than all others. How could society fail to perish if, while the political bond is relaxed, the moral bond were not tightened? And what makes a people master of itself if it has not submitted to God?[33]

No longer must we fall for the worn-out trope of Jefferson's misunderstood phrase "separation of church and state" as constitutional. It isn't and never has been! (It certainly isn't and never has been as popularly understood.)

Crusaders of separation cry for a naked public square—one where faith is personal and private; belonging in the home and house of worship, not in the halls of power. They fear favoritism of one faith over another. And rightly so. But the establishment clause of the First Amendment wasn't meant to protect government from religion, rather religion from government.

A recognition of God and His blessings by the American people or by the few who walk the halls of power in no way establishes a law favoring one religion over another; or to put it bluntly: favoring Christianity—the religion most feared by liberals of the political and social cast—over secularism. What does the First Amendment say? *"Congress* shall make *no law* respecting an *establishment* of religion" (emphasis mine). Nor shall Congress prohibit "the *free* exercise thereof." The free exercise—whether in private or in public. What is needed in the United States is not a naked public square, where God is consigned to private and personal corners but a civil public square, where God may be spoken of without constraint . . . yet with civility.

No longer must we buy the nonsense that our nation's Founders were irreligious men whose sole intellectual motivation was the godlessness of the Enlightenment. They weren't, and it wasn't!

In fact, it is doubtful that even the most godless of our Founders, Thomas Paine, unlike many Progressives today, would go so far as to hope that every remnant of God's providence over America would be lost in the folds of dusty history books no longer read. Sensible as to the almost inseparable link between American character and religion, like Tocqueville who wrote about it sixty years later, Paine recorded in his famous pamphlet, *Common Sense*, this sentiment: "As to religion, I hold it to be the indispensable duty of all government to protect all conscientious professors thereof, and I know of no other business which government hath to do therewith."[34]

Governments need not dictate the conscience of their citizens, as was the case with the Crown and the Church of England in colonial America. But the United States government cannot dethrone religious conscience when it is brought to bear in the public square and call such action legal. We should never tolerate any attempt to oust our religious convictions when those convictions are expressed publicly. To do so is to betray our God and our forefathers.

Yet more is needed—something positive and practical. We must read and understand the Bible ourselves, just as our Founders did. They knew the Bible, quoted from it often, and tried to govern their lives by its precepts. This was true even of the Founders deemed irreligious, including Thomas Jefferson.

During his presidency, Jefferson, almost every Sunday morning, walked down Pennsylvania Avenue to attend services at Christ Church, which was then meeting in a converted tobacco barn on the southeast side of Capitol Hill. One Sunday morning, Jefferson bumped into a friend on the street who questioned Jefferson as to why he was headed to church. Here's how Reverend Ethan Allen recorded the conversation:

> President Jefferson was on his way to church [on] a Sunday morning with his large red prayer book under his arm when a friend querying him after their mutual good morning said, "Which way are you walking, Mr. Jefferson." To which he replied, "To church, Sir." "You going to church, Mr. J.? You do not believe a word of it." "Sir," said Mr. J. "no nation has ever yet existed or

been governed without religion. Nor can be. The Christian religion is the best religion that has ever been given to man, and I as chief magistrate of this nation am bound to give it the sanction of my example. Good morning, Sir."[35]

Like Jefferson, we must attend church for the sake of honoring and worshipping God. We must also pray. We must pray individually and privately; we must pray with our families; we must pray in the community of worship and in the fellowship of other believers. We must pray for ourselves, our loved ones, our churches, our leaders, our military, our cities, our states, and our country. We must pray in faith, believing that what James wrote 2,000 years ago remains true today: "The effective, fervent prayer of a righteous man avails much" (James 5:16 NKJV).

Returning to our God will require humility and submission. This will not be an easy task for proud Americans, but return we must if we wish our republic of liberty to live long.

A MORAL GOAL: PRACTICE VIRTUE

History's course has a way of converging political, economic, and philosophical domains to bring about great change—or at least the potential of great change. But if the right individuals are missing from the mix, history's course will diverge and simply roll on unobstructed as it has for eons. Fortunately for twenty-first century Americans, the late 1760s through the late 1780s produced a convergence with the right mixture of men, and history changed its course. During this unique period of history, our Founders, who are universally recognized as a unique group of men, the likes of which have rarely been seen, appeared on the historical stage. According to Gordon Wood, our Founding Fathers were unique because of their character. Wood wrote:

> These were men . . . [who] took the matter of character very, very seriously. They were the first generation in history that was self-consciously self-made, men who understood the arc of lives, as of nations, as being one of moral progress. They saw themselves as comprising the world's first true meritocracy.[36]

Character. Morality. Virtue.

Unless we mean to lose our liberty, we must restore and practice the virtues our Founders treasured: individual responsibility, hard work, self-sacrifice, frugality, respect, self-sufficiency, truth-telling, self-restraint, modesty, wisdom, justice, diligence, duty, grace, mercy, civility, courage, and patriotism. We must live these virtues and others like them every day of our lives and demand that our leaders do the same, or we must find other and better leaders to represent us and our nation.

During the years of Theodore Roosevelt's presidency he would, on occasion, take his sons Quentin and Archie and some of their chums on the presidential sloop down the Potomac. As the USS *Mayflower* passed Mount Vernon and George Washington's grave, Roosevelt would make the boys stand at attention at the rail while the ship's bell rang. Then he would give the boys a speech they had heard many times before but one worth hearing again. Roosevelt explained that the bell rang out in tribute to the soul of that great man:

> We're now passing his house, and the things he loved; his body, too, which he had to leave behind him. Wouldn't it be fine if you and I grew up to be

thus respected? Of course, you may not be able to get thousands to respect you, as Washington did; but you can begin by getting two or three — maybe six or a dozen — and that's fine too.[37]

Presidents (often) and congressmen (almost always) are not thus respected. And the loss of our liberty is the want of it. We deserve better. But since our elected leaders come from our ranks, we must be better.

At the age of fourteen, George Washington copied 110 maxims into a daybook to help him polish his manners and learn proper decorum in the company of others. He titled his book, *Rules of Civility & Decent Behaviour in Company and Conversation*. It is well worth reading . . . and rereading . . . and reading to your children. It is well worth your time to read about other great men and women in our country's history whose towering character is worthy of emulation. And then do it — follow in their footsteps.

Our forefathers were not made of sugar-candy. They did not establish and build America while lounging on feather beds, and America's glory cannot be reestablished in the ease of life. The restoration of American liberty will only be achieved by doing the hard work of living virtuous lives and passing these virtues to our posterity, teaching our children the value of living a life worth imitating.

The questions are yours to answer. How virtuous are you? Is your life worth following?

AN INTELLECTUAL GOAL: RECOVER HISTORY

It was mentioned earlier, but a reminder is helpful: the greatest danger to our country lies not without but within. And the surest way to destroy our country is to destroy its memory—its culture and its history.

Shortly after the delegates at the Constitutional Convention completed their work in 1787, James McHenry of Maryland recorded an exchange between an anxious Mrs. Powel and a witty Benjamin Franklin. Mrs. Powel cornered Franklin outside the Pennsylvania State House (now known as Independence Hall) and asked, "Well, Doctor, what have we got—a republic or a monarchy?" Franklin answered, "A republic, if you can keep it."[38]

And keeping a republic of liberty is not as easy as it seems.

The great republic of Rome fell into disrepair and became the Roman Empire, ruled under the tyranny of the Caesars. But not even an empire can endure forever without virtue. As scholar Adrian Goldsworthy observed, the Roman Empire fell from without, but only after it had fallen from within. "Long decline was the fate of the Roman Empire," he wrote. "In the end, it may well have been 'murdered' by barbarian invaders, but these struck at a body made vulnerable by prolonged decay."[39]

"Long decline" and "prolonged decay"—these are the results of inattention, forgetfulness, and cowardice.

The future is found in the past. And today, our amnesia of history threatens the hope of America long remaining liberty's land. Unless we recover our past, our future as a free people will fade into the hazy mist of days gone by. Like a corrosive acid eating away our nation's memory, our ignorance of history will reap consequences too terrible to contemplate—the plaguing doubt that our children and our children's children will live in an America more free and more prosperous than the America we have enjoyed. Our ever growing national debt threatens to enslave our children to perpetual economic troubles and increased confiscation by the state, preventing them the liberty to earn, keep, and invest their income as they see fit.

If the very foundation of freedom rots away, where will freedom find a home? We must shore up this foundation. We must rid ourselves of today's lies and repair our liberty with historic truths. We must appreciate the value of history by reading and heeding it. We must read and understand the founding documents: the Declaration of Independence, the Constitution, and the Bill of Rights. And with passion we must teach our children the value of history.

We must become more involved in our communities, educating ourselves about issues and candidates, committing to vote for those who uphold the principles of our founding, and working to ensure that those candidates are placed on the ballot—even if it means stepping into the arena ourselves.

We must love America enough to bear whatever sacrifices must be borne to protect and preserve liberty for ourselves and our posterity. E. B. White said it so beautifully: "To hold America in one's thoughts is like holding a love letter in one's hand—it has so special a meaning."[40] We must fall in love with America once again, by falling in love with her history.

However, merely conjuring up the spirit of 1776, 1787, or 1791 is not enough to push back against an ever encroaching government and reclaim our liberty. "Man . . . is not a crab," philosopher Marc Guerra wrote, "he cannot retreat backwards into the past in order to escape the problems of the present or those that threaten his future."[41]

We must not deceive ourselves by romanticizing the America of '76, '87, or '91 as a bygone age of gold or a lost Garden of Eden. It was not. But the timeless principles captured in the documents of those years, to say nothing of the lives of those who penned them and defended them, continue to endure in the hearts and minds of many Americans. Those principles may lie dormant, but there they lay, waiting for someone or something to awaken them. And once awakened, just as our Founders taught and lived, the historic truth that liberty is only secure in a land of virtue and truth will America once again shine like a city upon a hill.

So let us look to history to learn to awaken those principles. Let us study history to find a guide in renewing those principles. And let us apply the truths of history and re-found our republic.

Perhaps, if we dedicate ourselves to these three goals—to return to God, to become people of virtue, and to value our history—we might, in our day, do something worth remembering; we might live up to the expectations of our forefathers and our God. And in that glorious day, perhaps the cry will echo forth: *O America, thou did as God commanded and His blessings of liberty shall continue upon thee and thy children.*

—····✲····—

JOHN ADAMS, just a week before the pivotal vote on independence, sat down and penned a letter to his cousin, who was a pastor in Massachusetts, encouraging him to keep at the useful employment of "pulling down the Strong Holds of Satan."

> Statesmen, my dear Sir, may plan and speculate for Liberty, but it is Religion and Morality alone, which can establish the Principles upon which Freedom can securely stand. . . . The only foundation of a free Constitution, is pure Virtue, and if this cannot

be inspired into our People, in a greater Measure, than they have it now, They may change their Rulers, and the form of Government, but they will not obtain a lasting liberty.—They will only exchange Tyrants for Tyrannies.[42]

Freedom is one of the greatest gifts from the hand of God. Yet, it can also be one of the greatest curses. If we abuse our freedom through neglect and careless inattention to our religious and moral heritage, then the Lord may give us the freedom to run away from liberty . . . and headlong into the noose of tyranny. I know not what others will choose, but I refuse to abase my liberty and be choked off from my freedom. I choose to stand with Daniel Webster and all lovers of liberty—both today and tomorrow.

I shall stand by the Union, and by all who stand by it. I shall do justice to the whole country, according to the best of my ability, in all I say, and act for the good of the whole country in all I do. I mean to stand upon the Constitution. I need no other platform. I shall know but one country. The ends I aim at shall be my country's, my God's, and Truth's. . . . I was born an American; I live an American; I shall die an American; and I intend to perform the duties incumbent upon me in that character to the end of my career. I mean to do this, with absolute disregard of personal consequences. What are personal consequences? What is the individual man, with all the good or evil that may betide him, in comparison with the good or evil which may befall a great country in a crisis like this, and in the midst of great transactions which concern that country's fate? Let the consequences be what they will, I am careless. No man can suffer too much, and no man can fall too soon, if he suffer, or if he fall, in defense of the liberties and Constitution of his country.[43]

Patrick Henry would have thrilled at Webster's words. Henry, the man who cried, "Give me liberty or give me death," was in earnest in 1775—he would have given his life for liberty. And in a way he did. He gave the best years of his life for that very cause. When liberty was won in 1781, after the victory at Yorktown, Henry's friend, George Mason, wrote to him:

I congratulate you most sincerely on this the accomplishment of what I know was the warmest wish of your heart, the establishment of American independence and the liberty of our country. We are now to rank among the nations of the world; but whether our independence shall prove a blessing or a curse must depend upon our own wisdom or folly, virtue or wickedness.[44]

Today is *the day*—the day we shall stand or fall, demonstrate wisdom or folly, be virtuous or wicked. Today is the day. Who shall stand with me?

The choice is yours. All that hangs in the balance are the blessings of liberty. Will you stand for liberty? Will you secure liberty for your posterity so they may taste freedom and know the art of living free?

The questions are of vital import, for what was written long ago remains true today: "a Constitution of Government once changed from Freedom, can never be restored. Liberty once lost is lost forever."[45]

—·····❋·····—

The
APPENDICES

THE BATTLE OVER THE FOUNDERS' VISION of America has
raged for years and rages still. America had barely secured
her independence from Great Britain when the contro-
versy began. One group of Founders, known as Federalists,
wanted a consolidated and stronger central government.
Another group, just as patriotic and vital to American
liberty, Antifederalists, wanted a diffused and weaker pro-
vincial government. The Federalists won this dispute with
the adoption of the United States Constitution, but the
question remains: who were the real guardians of the spirit
of '76 and '87 and '91?

The Founders were not, as some suppose, of like mind
on every detail of government or the meaning of America.
They fought, held petty grudges, and often acted small.
They were, after all, mere men. But they were like-minded
on the central issues of liberty and tyranny. And on these,
there was no deviation. America would be free if her

people would be virtuous, and they would be virtuous if they would be religious.

O America! provides sufficient proof that the Founders' formula for freedom was the liberty triangle. However, lest anyone doubt the truth of this claim, the following quotations from the Founders' own pens (with their sometimes unique spelling) and voices, as well as George Washington's Farewell Address, should dispel all disbelief.

APPENDIX I

QUOTATIONS

—꙳꙳꙳✖꙳꙳꙳—

THOUGHTS *on* AMERICA

The American union will last as long as God pleases. It is the duty of every American Citizen to exert his utmost abilities and endeavors to preserve it as long as possible and to pray with submission to Providence "esto perpetua" ["may it last forever"].

—JOHN ADAMS in a letter to Charles Carroll
August 2, 1820

—꙳꙳꙳✖꙳꙳꙳—

I wish we were a more religious People.

–Samuel Adams in a letter to Elizabeth Adams

December 9, 1776

Our Independence, I think, is secured. Whether America shall long preserve her Freedom or not, will depend on her Virtue.

–Samuel Adams

December 21, 1778

The American Revolution was the grand operation, which seemed to be assigned by the Deity to the men of this age in our country.

–Patrick Henry in a letter to Henry Lee

June 27, 1795

To one however who adores liberty, and the noble virtues of which it is the parent, there is some consolation in seeing, while we lament the fall of British liberty, the rise of that of America. Yes, my friend, like a young phoenix she will rise full plumed and glorious from her mother's ashes.

−ARTHUR LEE in a letter to Samuel Adams
December 24, 1772

—✦—

May we ever be a people favoured of God. May our land be a land of liberty, the seat of virtue, the asylum of the oppressed, a name and a praise in the whole earth, until the last shock of time shall bury the empires of the world in one common undistinguished ruin!

−JOSEPH WARREN
Boston Massacre Oration
March 5, 1772

—✦—

The wisdom and justice of the American governments, and the virtue of the inhabitants, may, if they are not deficient in the improvement of their own advantages, render the United States of America an enviable example to all the world, of peace, liberty, righteousness, and truth.

— MERCY OTIS WARREN
History of the Rise, Progress and Termination of the
America Revolution
1805

—⸗✳⸗—

The man must be bad indeed, who can look upon the events of the American Revolution without feeling the warmest gratitude towards the great Author of the Universe whose divine interposition was so frequently manifested in our behalf.

— GEORGE WASHINGTON in a letter to Samuel Langdon
September 28, 1789

—⸗✳⸗—

The establishment of our new Government seemed to be the last great experiment for promoting human happiness.

—GEORGE WASHINGTON in a letter to
Catherine Macaulay Graham
January 9, 1790

—····✿····—

THOUGHTS *on* LIBERTY

Yesterday the greatest Question was decided, which ever was debated in America, and a greater perhaps, never was or will be decided among Men. A Resolution was passed without one dissenting Colony "that these united Colonies, are, and of right ought to be free and independent States, and as such, they have, and of Right ought to have full Power to make War, conclude Peace, establish Commerce, and to do all other Acts and Things, which other States may rightfully do." You will see in a few days a Declaration setting forth the Causes, which have impell'd Us to this mighty Revolution, and the Reasons which will justify it, in the Sight of God and Man. A Plan of Confederation will be taken up in a few days.

—JOHN ADAMS in a letter to Abigail Adams
July 3, 1776 (morning)

—*✵*—

The Delay of this Declaration to this Time, has many great Advantages attending it. The Hopes of Reconciliation, which were fondly entertained by Multitudes of honest and well meaning tho weak and mistaken People, have been gradually and at last totally extinguished. Time has been given for the whole People, maturely to consider, the great Question of Independence and to ripen their Judgments, dissipate their Fears, and allure their Hopes, by discussing it in News Papers and Pamphletts, by debating it, in Assemblies Conventions, Committees of safety and Inspection in Town and County Meetings, as well as in private Conversation, so that the whole People in every Colony of the 13, have now adopted it, as their own Act.

This will cement the Union, and avoid those Hearts and perhaps Convulsions which might have been occasioned, by such a Declaration Six Months ago. ¶ But the day is past. The Second Day of July 1776, will be the most memorable Epocha, in the History of America. I am apt to believe that it will be celebrated, by succeeding Generations, as the great anniversary Festival. It ought to be commemorated, as the Day of Deliverance by solemn Acts of Devotion to God Almighty. It ought to be solemnized with Pomp and Parade with shews, Games, Sports, Guns, Bells, Bonfires and Illuminations from one End of this Continent to the other from this Time forward forever more. ¶ You may think me transported with Enthusiasm, but I am not. I am well aware of the Toil and Blood and Treasure, that it will cost Us to maintain this Declaration, and support and defend these states. Yet through all the Gloom I can see the Rays of ravishing Light and Glory. I can see that the End is more than worth all the Means. and that Posterity will tryumph in the Days Transaction, even altho We should rue it, which I trust in God We shall not.

—JOHN ADAMS in a letter to Abigail Adams
July 3, 1776 (evening)

—····❊····—

A general dissolution of the principles and manners will more surely overthrow the liberties of America than the whole force of the common enemy. While the people are virtuous, they cannot be subdued; but when once they lose their virtue, they will be ready to surrender their liberties to the first external or internal invader.

—SAMUEL ADAMS in a letter to James Warren
February 12, 1779

—····※····—

It was asked in the Reign of Charles the 2d of England, How shall we turn the Minds of the People from the Attention to their Liberties? The Answer was, by making them extravagant, luxurious, effeminate.

—SAMUEL ADAMS in a letter to John Scollay
December 30, 1780

—····※····—

Those who would give up essential liberty to purchase a little temporary safety deserve neither liberty nor safety.

−Benjamin Franklin
Speech to the Pennsylvania Assembly
November 11, 1755

—⁕—

The God who gave us life, gave us liberty at the same time; the hand of force may destroy, but cannot disjoin them.

−Thomas Jefferson
"A Summary View of the Rights of British America"
1774

—⁕—

These are the times that try men's souls. The summer soldier and the sunshine patriot will, in this crisis, shrink from the service of their country; but he that stands by it now, deserves the love and thanks of man and woman. Tyranny, like hell, is not easily conquered; yet we have this consolation with us, that the harder the conflict, the more glorious the triumph. What we obtain too cheep, we esteem too lightly: it is dearness only that gives every thing its value. Heaven knows how to put a proper price upon its goods; and it would be strange indeed if so celestial an article as freedom should not be highly rated.

–THOMAS PAINE
The American Crisis
December 25, 1776

—''''✗''''—

The establishment of Civil and Religious Liberty was the Motive which induced me to the Field—the object is attained—and it now remains to be my earnest wish & prayer, that the Citizens of the United States could make a wise and virtuous use of the blessings placed before them.

–GEORGE WASHINGTON in a letter to the Reformed German Congregation of New York City
November 27, 1783

—''''✗''''—

There is not a single instance in history in which civil liberty was lost and religious liberty preserved entire. If therefore we yield up our temporal property, we at the same time deliver the conscience into bondage.

—JOHN WITHERSPOON
"The Dominion of Providence Over the Passions of Men"
May 17, 1776

—····※····—

THOUGHTS *on* RELIGION *and* VIRTUE

When public virtue is gone, when the national spirit is fled . . . the republic is lost in essence, though it may still exist in form.

—JOHN ADAMS in a letter to Benjamin Rush
1808

—····※····—

I have long been convincd that our Enemies have made it an Object, to eradicate from the Minds of the People in general a Sense of true Religion & Virtue, in hopes thereby the more easily to carry their Point of enslaving them. Indeed my Friend, this is a Subject so important in my Mind, that I know not how to leave it. Revelation assures us that "Righteousness exalteth a Nation"—Communities are dealt with in this World by the wise and just Ruler of the Universe. The diminution of publick Virtue is usually attended with that of publick Happiness, and the publick Liberty will not long survive the total Extinction of Morals. "The Roman Empire, says the Historian, *must* have sunk, though the Goths had not invaded it. Why ? Because the Roman Virtue was sunk." Could I be assured that America would remain virtuous, I would venture to defy the utmost Efforts of Enemies to subjugate her. You will allow me to remind you, that the Morals of that City which has born so great a Share of the American Contest, depend much upon the Vigilance of the respectable Body of Magistrates of which you are a Member.

—SAMUEL ADAMS in a letter to John Scollay

April 30, 1776

There are Virtues & Vices which are properly call political. "Corruption, Dishonesty to one's Country Luxury and Extravagance tend to the Ruin of States." ¶ . . . He who is void of virtuous Attachments in private Life, is, or very soon will be void of all Regard for his Country. There is seldom an Instance of a Man guilty of betraying his Country, who had not before lost the Feeling of moral Obligations in his private Connections. Before [Dr. Benjamin Church, Jr.] was detected of holding a criminal Correspondence with the Enemies of his Country, his Infidelity to his Wife had been notorious. Since private and publick Vices, are in Reality, though not always apparently, so nearly connected, of how much Importance, how necessary is it, that the utmost Pains, be taken by the Publick, to have the Principles of Virtues early inculcated on the Minds even of Children, and the moral Sense kept alive, and that the wise Institutions of our Ancestors for these great Purposes encouragd by the Government.

−SAMUEL ADAMS in a letter to James Warren

February 12, 1779

—••••✖••••—

Only a virtuous people are capable of freedom. As nations become corrupt and vicious, they have more need of masters.

—BENJAMIN FRANKLIN in a letter to Messrs. The Abbes
Chalut and Arnaud
April 17, 1787

———※———

Truth, honor, and religion are the only foundation to build human happiness upon. They never fail to yield a mind solid satisfaction; For conscious virtue gives pleasure to the soul.

—NATHANAEL GREENE in a letter to
Catharine Ward Greene
1776

———※———

The politician who loves liberty sees . . . a gulph that may swallow up the liberty to which he is devoted. He knows that morality overthrown (and morality *must* fall without religion) the terrors of despotism can alone curb the impetuous passions of man, and confine him within the bounds of social duty.

—ALEXANDER HAMILTON
The Stand, no. 3
April 7, 1798

—◊◊◊◊※◊◊◊◊—

The great pillars of all government and of social life,— I mean virtue, morality, and religion. This is the armor, my friend, and this alone, that renders us invincible. These are the tactics we should study. If we lose these, we are conquered, fallen indeed.

—PATRICK HENRY in a letter to Archibald Blair
January 8, 1799

—◊◊◊◊※◊◊◊◊—

Is there no virtue among us? If there be not, we are in a wretched situation. No theoretical checks—no form of government can render us secure. To suppose that any form of government will secure liberty or happiness without any virtue in the people, is a chimerical idea. If there be sufficient virtue and intelligence in the community, it will be exercised in the selection of these men. So that we do not depend on their virtue, or put confidence in our rulers, but in the people who are to choose them.

−James Madison
Speech to the Virginia Ratifying Convention
June 20, 1788

—⁊⁊⁊⁊※⁊⁊⁊⁊—

As there is a degree of depravity in mankind which requires a certain degree of circumspection and distrust: So there are other qualities in human nature, which justify a certain portion of esteem and confidence. Republican government presupposes the existence of these qualities in a higher degree than any other form. Were the picture which have been drawn by the political jealousy of some among us, faithful likenesses of the human character, the inference would be that there is not sufficient virtue among men for self-government; and that nothing less than the chains of despotism can restrain them from destroying and devouring one another.

—JAMES MADISON
The Federalist Papers, No. 55
1788

—·····✸·····—

Illustrious examples are displayed to our view that we may imitate as well as admire. Before we can be distinguished by the same honors, we must be distinguished by the same virtues. What are those virtues? They are chiefly the same virtues, which we have already seen to be descriptive of the American character—the love of liberty, and the love of law.

—JAMES WILSON
Of the Study of the Law in the United States
c. 1790

—·····✸·····—

He is the best friend to American liberty, who is most sincere and active in promoting true and undefiled religion, and who sets himself with the greatest firmness to bear down prophanity and immorality of every kind. Whoever is an avowed enemy to God, I scruple not to call him an enemy to his country.

—John Witherspoon
"The Dominion of Providence Over the Passions of Men"
May 17, 1776

The United States in Congress assembled . . . do further recommend to all ranks, to testify their gratitude to God for his goodness, by a cheerful obedience to his laws, and by promoting, each in his station, and by his influence, the practice of true and undefiled religion, which is the great foundation of public prosperity and national happiness.

—John Witherspoon
Thanksgiving Day Proclamation
October 11, 1782

APPENDIX II

GEORGE WASHINGTON'S FAREWELL ADDRESS

—◦◦◦❋◦◦◦—

FROM THE BEGINNING OF THE AMERICAN REPUBLIC, George Washington was the embodiment of America herself. He led the Continental Army for eight years (1775–1783), mostly through defeat, to the glorious victory at Yorktown and independence. He shepherded a contentious Constitutional Convention, as the presiding officer, in developing the document that birthed the American republic. He served as the first president and the only president elected unanimously—twice (1789 and 1792).

Expressing a desire to retire to his "vine and fig tree" at Mt. Vernon, President Washington approached Alexander Hamilton, the Secretary of Treasury, in February 1796 about writing a valedictorian document. Washington, approaching his mid-sixties, wanted to retire because he was simply tired and worn out. But he was also deeply wounded by critical newspaper editors who accused him of setting up a quasi-monarchy. In some corners of the country he was called "George IV" in succession of England's defeated king George III. By retiring, Washington hoped to silence the wagging tongues of monarchy and state unequivocally that the office of the presidency outlives the man.

Since the publication of Washington's Farewell Address, historians have studied the language to determine who wrote the document. Without a doubt, it was an amalgamation. Some of the expressions were James Madison's; most of the phrases were Alexander Hamilton's; all the opinions were George Washington's. Hamilton took the lead in capturing Washington's judgments and language, but Madison gave Washington the idea to publish the document as a direct address to the people of America. Following Madison's advice, Washington chose David C. Claypoole's *American Daily Advertiser* to publish the letter. It appeared in the September 19, 1796, edition. Copies of Washington's letter found its way into other newspapers in subsequent weeks and became commonly known as "Washington's Farewell Address" in the *Courier of New Hampshire*. Ironically, the Farewell Address was never delivered as a farewell address—only as a speech. It was an open letter to the American people and should rightly be called Washington's Farewell Letter.

Washington had three purposes in writing the letter. He wanted to announce his retirement, encourage unity at home, and advocate for independence abroad. It is often mistakenly thought that Washington, in laying out his warning against being caught up in European squabbles, coined the famous phrase, "entangling alliances." He did not; Thomas Jefferson did in his first Inaugural in 1801.

Washington left Philadelphia, and the presidency, on March 4, 1797, and returned home to set upon a system of crop rotations and to tend his trees. Washington didn't enjoy his "vine and fig tree" long; he died on December 14, 1799.

—٭—

TO THE PEOPLE OF THE UNITED STATES —

FRIENDS AND FELLOW CITIZENS: The period for a new election of a citizen, to administer the executive government of the United States, being not far distant, and the time actually arrived when your thoughts must be employed in designating the person who is to be clothed with that important trust, it appears to me proper, especially as it may conduce to a more distinct expression of the public voice, that I should now apprise you of the resolution I have formed, to decline being considered among the number of those out of whom a choice is to be made.

I beg you, at the same time, to do me the justice to be assured that this resolution has not been taken without a strict regard to all the considerations appertaining to the relation which binds a dutiful citizen to his country, and that, in withdrawing the tender of service which silence in my situation might imply, I am influenced by no diminution of zeal for your future interest, no deficiency of grateful respect for your past kindness; but am supported by a full conviction that the step is compatible with both.

The acceptance of, and continuance hitherto in, the office to which your suffrages have twice called me have been a uniform sacrifice of inclination to the opinion of duty, and to a deference for what appeared to be your desire. I constantly hoped that it would have been much earlier in my power, consistently with motives which I was not at liberty to disregard, to return to that retirement from which I had been reluctantly drawn. The strength of my inclination to do this, previous to the last election, had even led to the preparation of an address to declare it to you; but mature reflection on the then perplexed and critical posture of our affairs with foreign nations, and the unanimous advice of persons entitled to my confidence, impelled me to abandon the idea.

I rejoice that the state of your concerns, external as well as internal, no longer renders the pursuit of inclination incompatible with the sentiment of duty or propriety, and am persuaded whatever partiality may be retained for my services, that in the present circumstances of our country, you will not disapprove my determination to retire.

The impressions, with which I first undertook the arduous trust, were explained on the proper occasion. In the discharge of this trust I will only say, that I have with good intentions contributed towards the organization and administration of the government, the best exertions of which a very fallible judgment was capable.

Not unconscious, in the outset, of the inferiority of my qualifications, experience, in my own eyes, perhaps still more in the eyes of others, has strengthened the motives to diffidence of myself; and every day the increasing weight of years admonishes me more and more that the shade of retirement is as necessary to me as it will be welcome. Satisfied that if any circumstances have given peculiar value to my services, they were temporary, I have the consolation to believe, that while choice and prudence invite me to quit the political scene, patriotism does not forbid it.

In looking forward to the moment which is intended to terminate the career of my public life, my feelings do not permit me to suspend the deep acknowledgment of that debt of gratitude which I owe to my beloved country, for the many honors it has conferred upon me; still more for the steadfast confidence with which it has supported me; and for the opportunities I have thence enjoyed of manifesting my inviolable attachment, by services, faithful and persevering, though in usefulness unequal to my zeal. If benefits have resulted to our country from these services, let it always be remembered to your praise, and as an instructive example in our annals, that under circumstances in which the passions, agitated in every direction, were liable to mislead, amidst appearances sometimes dubious, vicissitudes of fortune often discouraging, in situations in which not unfrequently want of success has countenanced the spirit of criticism, the constancy of your support was the essential prop of the efforts, and the guarantee of the plans by which they were effected. Profoundly penetrated with this idea, I shall carry it with me to my grave, as a strong incitement to unceasing wishes that heaven may continue to you the choicest tokens of its beneficence; that your union and brotherly affection may be perpetual; that the free Constitution, which is the work of your hands, may be sacredly maintained; that its administration, in every department, may be stamped with wisdom and virtue; that, in fine, the happiness of the people of these States, under the auspices of liberty, may be made complete by so careful a preservation and so prudent a use of this blessing as will acquire to them the glory of recommending it to the applause, the affection, and adoption of every nation which is yet a stranger to it.

Here, perhaps, I ought to stop. But a solicitude for your welfare, which cannot end but with my life, and the apprehension of danger, natural to that solicitude, urge me on an occasion like the present to offer to your solemn contemplation, and to recommend to your frequent review, some sentiments which are the result of much reflection, of no inconsiderable observation, and which appear to me all important to the permanency of your felicity as a people. These will be offered to you with the more freedom, as you can only see in them the disinterested warnings of a parting friend, who can possibly have no personal motive to bias his counsel. Nor can I forget, as an encouragement to it, your indulgent reception of my sentiments of a former and not dissimilar occasion.

Interwoven as is the love of liberty with every ligament of your hearts, no recommendation of mine is necessary to fortify or confirm the attachment.

The unity of government which constitutes you one people is also now dear to you. It is justly so; for it is a main pillar in the edifice of your real independence, the support of your tranquility at home, your peace abroad, of your safety, of your prosperity, of that very liberty which you so highly prize. But as it is easy to foresee that from different causes and from different quarters, much pains will be taken, many artifices employed, to weaken in your minds the conviction of this truth; as this is the point in your political fortress against which the batteries of internal and external enemies will be most constantly and actively (though often covertly and insidiously) directed, it is of infinite moment that you should properly estimate the immense value of your national union to your collective and immovable attachment to it; accustoming yourselves to think and speak of its preservation with jealous anxiety; discountenancing whatever may suggest even a suspicion that it can in any event be abandoned; and indignantly frowning upon the first dawning of every attempt to alienate any portion of our country from the rest, or to enfeeble the sacred ties which now link together the various parts.

For this you have every inducement of sympathy and interest. Citizens by birth or choice, of a common country, that country has a right to concentrate your affections. The name of American, which belongs to you, in your national capacity, must always exalt the just pride of patriotism, more than any appellation derived from local discriminations. With slight shades of difference, you have the same religion, manners, habits, and political principles. You have in a common cause fought and triumphed together. The independence and liberty you possess are the work of joint councils and joint efforts, of common dangers, sufferings, and successes.

But these considerations, however powerfully they address themselves to your sensibility, are greatly outweighed by those which apply more immediately to your interest. Here every portion of our country finds the most commanding motives for carefully guarding and preserving the union of the whole.

The North, in an unrestrained intercourse with the South, protected by the equal laws of a common government, finds in the productions of the latter great additional resources of maritime and commercial enterprise and precious materials of manufacturing industry. The South, in the same intercourse, benefiting by the agency of the North, sees its agriculture grow and its commerce expand. Turning partly into its own channels the seamen of the North, it finds its particular navigation invigorated; and while it contributes, in different ways, to nourish and increase the general mass of the national navigation, it looks forward to the protection of a maritime strength, to which itself is unequally adapted. The East, in like intercourse with the West, already finds and, in the progressive improvement of interior communications, by land and water, will more and more find a valuable vent for the commodities which it brings from abroad, or manufactures at home. The West derives from the East supplies requisite to its growth and comfort, and what is perhaps of still greater consequence, it must of necessity owe the secure enjoyment of indispensable outlets for its own productions to the weight, influence, and the future maritime strength of the Atlantic side of the union, directed by an indissoluble community of interest as one nation. Any other tenure by which the West can hold this essential advantage, whether derived from its own separate strength or from an apostate and unnatural connection with any foreign power, must be intrinsically precarious.

While, then, every part of our country thus feels an immediate and particular interest in union, all the parts combined cannot fail to find in the united mass of means and efforts greater strength, greater resource, proportionably greater security from external danger, a less frequent interruption of their peace by foreign nations; and, what is of inestimable value, they must derive from union an exemption from those broils and wars between themselves, which so frequently afflict neighboring countries not tied together by the same government which their own rivalships alone would be sufficient to produce, but which opposite foreign alliances, attachments, and intrigues would stimulate and embitter. Hence, likewise, they will avoid the necessity of those overgrown military establishments which under any form of government are inauspicious to liberty, and which are to be regarded as particularly hostile to republican liberty: in this sense it is that your union ought to be considered as a main prop of your liberty, and that the love of the one ought to endear to you the preservation of the other.

These considerations speak a persuasive language to every reflecting and virtuous mind, and exhibit the continuance of the Union as a primary object of patriotic desire. Is there a doubt, whether a common government can embrace so large a sphere? Let experience solve it. To listen to mere speculation in such a case were criminal. We are authorized to hope that a proper organization of the whole, with the auxiliary agency of governments for the respective subdivisions, will afford a happy issue to the experiment. 'Tis well worth a fair and full experiment. With such powerful and obvious motives to union, affecting all parts of our country, while experience shall not have demonstrated its impracticability, there will always be reason to distrust the patriotism of those who, in any quarter, may endeavor to weaken its bands.

In contemplating the causes which may disturb our union, it occurs, as a matter of serious concern, that any ground should have been furnished for characterizing parties by geographical discriminations — Northern and Southern, Atlantic and Western — whence designing men may endeavor to excite a belief that there is a real difference of local interests and views. One of the expedients of party to acquire influence within particular districts is to misrepresent the opinions and aims of other districts. You cannot shield yourselves too much against the jealousies and heart-burning which spring from these misrepresentations; they then to render alien to each other those who ought to be bound together by fraternal affection. The inhabitants of our western country have lately had a useful lesson on this head. They have seen, in the negotiation by the executive, and in the unanimous ratification by the Senate, of the treaty with Spain, and in the universal satisfaction of that event throughout the United States, a decisive proof how unfounded were the suspicions propagated among them of a policy in the general government and in the Atlantic States, unfriendly to their interests in regard to the Mississippi; they have been witnesses to the formation of two treaties—that with Great Britain and that with Spain—which secure to them everything they could desire, in respect to our foreign relations, towards confirming their prosperity. Will it not be their wisdom to rely, for the preservation of these advantages, on the union by which they were procured? Will they not henceforth be deaf to those advisers, if such there are, who would sever them from their brethren, and connect them with aliens?

To the efficacy and permanency of your union, a government for the whole is indispensable. No alliances, however strict, between the parts, can be an adequate substitute; they must inevitably experience the infractions and interruptions, which alliances, in all times, have experienced. Sensible of this momentous truth, you have improved upon your first essay by the adoption of a constitution of government better calculated than your former for an intimate union, and for the efficacious management of your common concerns. This government, the offspring of our own choice, uninfluenced and unawed, adopted upon full investigation and mature deliberation, completely free in its principles, in the distribution of its powers, uniting security with energy, and containing within itself a provision for its own amendment, has just claim to your confidence and your support. Respect for its authority, compliance with its laws, acquiescence in its measures, are duties enjoined by the fundamental maxims of true liberty. The basis of our political systems is the right of the people to make and to alter the constitutions of government. But the Constitution, which at any time exists, until changed by an explicit and authentic act of the whole people, is sacredly obligatory upon all. The very idea of the power and the right of the people to establish a government presupposes the duty of every individual to obey the established government.

All obstructions to the execution of the laws, all combinations and associations, under whatever plausible character, with the real design to direct, control, counteract, or awe the regular deliberation and action of the constituted authorities, are destructive of this fundamental principle and of fatal tendency. They serve to organize faction, to give it an artificial and extraordinary force; to put in the place of the delegated will of the nation, the will of a party, often a small but artful and enterprising minority of the community; and, according to the alternate triumphs of different parties, to make the public administration the mirror of the ill-concerted and incongruous projects of faction, rather than the organ of consistent and wholesome plans digested by common councils and modified by mutual interest.

However combinations or associations of the above description may now and then answer popular ends, they are likely, in the course of time and things, to become potent engines, by which cunning, ambitious, and unprincipled men will be enabled to subvert the power of the people, and to usurp for themselves the reins of government destroying afterwards the very engines which have lifted them to unjust dominion.

Toward the preservation of your government and the permanency of your present happy state, it is requisite, not only that you speedily discountenance irregular opposition to its acknowledged authority, but also that you resist with care the spirit of innovation upon its principles, however specious the pretexts. One method of assault may be to effect, in the forms of the constitution, alterations which will impair the energy of the system, and thus to undermine what cannot be directly overthrown. In all the changes to which you may be invited, remember that time and habit are at least as necessary to fix the true character of governments as of other human institutions; that experience is the surest standard by which to test the real tendency of the existing constitution of a country; that facility in changes, upon the credit of mere hypothesis and opinion, exposes to perpetual change, from the endless variety of hypothesis and opinion. And remember especially, that for the efficient management of your common interests, in a country so extensive as ours, a government of as much vigor as is consistent with the perfect security of liberty, is indispensable. Liberty itself will find in such a government, with powers properly distributed and adjusted, its surest guardian. It is, indeed, little else than a name, where the government is too feeble to withstand the enterprises of faction; to confine each member of society within the limits prescribed by the laws, and to maintain all in the secure and tranquil enjoyment of the rights of person and property.

I have already intimated to you the danger of parties in the state, with particular reference to the founding of them on geographical discriminations. Let me now take a more comprehensive view, and warn you in the most solemn manner against the baneful effects of the spirit of party, generally.

This spirit, unfortunately, is inseparable from our nature, having its root in the strongest passions of the human mind. It exists under different shapes in all governments, more or less stifled, controlled, or repressed; but in those of the popular form it is seen in its greatest rankness and is truly their worst enemy.

The alternate domination of one faction over another, sharpened by the spirit of revenge natural to party dissension, which in different ages and countries has perpetrated the most horrid enormities, is itself a frightful despotism. But this leads at length to a more formal and permanent despotism. The disorders and miseries which result gradually incline the minds of men to seek security and repose in the absolute power of an individual: and sooner or later the chief of some prevailing faction more able or more fortunate than his competitors, turns this disposition to the purposes of his own elevation, on the ruins of public liberty.

Without looking forward to an extremity of this kind, (which, nevertheless, ought not to be entirely out of sight,) the common and continual mischiefs of the spirit of party are sufficient to make it the interest and duty of a wise people to discourage and restrain it.

It serves always to distract the public councils, and enfeeble the public administration. It agitates the community with ill-founded jealousies and false alarms; kindles the animosity of one part against another; foments occasionally riot and insurrection. It opens the door to foreign influence and corruption, which find a facilitated access to the government itself, through the channels of party passion. Thus the policy and the will of one country are subjected to the policy and will of another.

There is an opinion that parties in free countries are useful checks upon the administration of the government and serve to keep alive the spirit of liberty. This within certain limits is probably true, and in governments of a monarchical cast patriotism may look with indulgence, if not with favor, upon the spirit of party. But in those of the popular character, in governments purely elective, it is a spirit not to be encouraged. From their natural tendency, it is certain there will always be enough of that spirit for every salutary purpose. And there being constant danger of excess, the effort ought to be, by force of public opinion, to mitigate and assuage it. A fire not to be quenched, it demands a uniform vigilance to prevent its bursting into a flame, lest, instead of warming, it should consume.

It is important, likewise, that the habits of thinking, in a free country, should inspire caution in those entrusted with its administration, to confine themselves within their respective constitutional spheres, avoiding, in the exercise of the powers of one department, to encroach upon another. The spirit of encroachment tends to consolidate the powers of the departments in one, and thus to create, whatever the form of government, a real despotism. A just estimate of that love of power, and proneness to abuse it, which predominates in the human heart, is sufficient to satisfy us of the truth of this position. The necessity of reciprocal checks in the exercise of political power, by dividing and distributing it into different depositaries, and constituting each the guardian of the public weal against invasion by the other, has been evinced by experiments ancient and modern: some of them in our country, and under our own eyes. To preserve them must be as necessary as to institute them. If, in the opinion of the people, the distribution or modification of the constitutional powers, be, in any particular, wrong, let it be corrected by an amendment in the way which the Constitution designates. But let there be no change by usurpation; for though this, in one instance, may be the instrument of good, it is the customary weapon by which free governments are destroyed. The precedent must always greatly overbalance, in permanent evil, and partial or transient benefit which the use can at any time yield.

Of all the dispositions and habits which lead to political prosperity, religion and morality are indispensable supports. In vain would that man claim the tribute of patriotism who should labor to subvert these great pillars of human happiness, these firmest props of the duties of men and citizens. The mere politician, equally with the pious man, ought to respect and to cherish them. A volume could not trace all their connections with private and public felicity. Let it simply be asked: where is the security for property, for reputation, for life, if the sense of religious obligation desert the oaths which are the instruments of investigation in courts of justice? And let us with caution indulge the supposition that morality can be maintained without religion. Whatever may be conceded to the influence of refined education on minds of peculiar structure, reason and experience both forbid us to expect that national morality can prevail in exclusion of religious principle.

'Tis substantially true that virtue or morality is a necessary spring of popular government. The rule indeed extends with more or less force to every species of free government. Who that is a sincere friend to it can look with indifference upon attempts to shake the foundations of the fabric?

Promote, then, as an object of primary importance, institutions for the general diffusion of knowledge. In proportion as the structure of a government gives force to public opinion, it is essential that public opinion should be enlightened.

As a very important source of strength and security, cherish public credit. One method of preserving it is to use it as sparingly as possible: avoiding occasions of expense by cultivating peace, but remembering also that timely disbursements to prepare for danger frequently prevent much greater disbursements to repel it; avoiding likewise the accumulation of debt, not only by shunning occasions of expense but by vigorous exertions in time of peace to discharge the debts which unavoidable war may have occasioned, not ungenerously throwing upon posterity the burden which we ourselves ought to bear. The execution of these maxims belongs to your representatives, but it is necessary that public opinion should cooperate. To facilitate to them the performance of their duty, it is essential that you should practically bear in mind that towards the payment of debts there must be revenue; that to have revenue there must be taxes; that no taxes can be devised which are not more or less inconvenient and unpleasant; that the intrinsic embarrassment, inseparable from the selection of the proper objects (which is always the choice of difficulties) ought to be a decisive motive for a candid construction of the conduct of the government in making it, and for a spirit of acquiescence in the measures for obtaining revenue which the public exigencies may at any time dictate.

Observe good faith and justice towards all nations. Cultivate peace and harmony with all. Religion and morality enjoin this conduct; and can it be that good policy does not equally enjoin it? It will be worthy of a free, enlightened, and, at no distant period, a great nation to give to mankind the magnanimous and too novel example of a people always guided by an exalted justice and benevolence. Who can doubt that in the course of time and things the fruits of such a plan would richly repay any temporary advantages which might be lost by a steady adherence to it? Can it be, that Providence has not connected the permanent felicity of a nation with its virtue? The experiment, at least, is recommended by every sentiment which ennobles human nature. Alas! is it rendered impossible by its vices?

In the execution of such a plan nothing is more essential than that permanent, inveterate antipathies against particular nations and passionate attachments for others should be excluded, and that in place of them just and amicable feelings towards all should be cultivated. The nation which indulges towards another an habitual hatred, or an habitual fondness, is in some degree a slave. It is a slave to its animosity or to its affection, either of which is sufficient to lead it astray from its duty and its interest. Antipathy in one nation against another disposes each more readily to offer insult and injury, to lay hold of slight causes of umbrage, and to be haughty and intractable, when accidental or trifling occasions of dispute occur. Hence frequent collisions, obstinate, envenomed, and bloody contests. The nation prompted by ill will and resentment sometimes impels to war the government, contrary to the best calculations of policy. The government sometimes participates in the national propensity, and adopts through passion what reason would reject; at other times, it makes the animosity of the nation subservient to projects of hostility instigated by pride, ambition, and other sinister and pernicious motives. The peace often, sometimes perhaps the liberty, of nations has been the victim.

So likewise, a passionate attachment of one nation for another produces a variety of evils. Sympathy for the favorite nation, facilitating the illusion of an imaginary common interest, in cases where no real common interest exists, and infusing into one the enmities of the other, betrays the former into a participation in the quarrels and wars of the latter, without adequate inducement or justification. It leads also to concessions to the favorite nation making the concessions; by unnecessarily parting with what ought to have been retained; and by exciting jealousy, ill will, and a disposition to retaliate, in the parties from whom equal privileges are withheld. And it gives to ambitious, corrupted, or deluded citizens (who devote themselves to the favorite nation) facility to betray or sacrifice the interests of their own country, without odium, sometimes even with popularity; gilding, with the appearances of a virtuous sense of obligation, a commendable deference for public opinion, or laudable zeal for public good, the base or foolish compliances of ambition, corruption, or infatuation.

As avenues to foreign influence, in innumerable ways, such attachments are particularly alarming to the truly enlightened and independent patriot. How many opportunities do they afford to tamper with domestic factions; to practice the arts of seduction; to mislead public opinion; to influence or awe the public councils! Such an attachment of a small or weak nation, toward a great and powerful one, dooms the former to be the satellite of the latter.

Against the insidious wiles of foreign influence (I conjure you to believe me, fellow citizens), the jealousy of a free people ought to be constantly awake, since history and experience prove that foreign influence is one of the most baneful foes of republican government. But that jealousy to be useful must be impartial; else it becomes the instrument of the very influence to be avoided, instead of a defense against it. Excessive partiality for one foreign nation, and excessive dislike of another, cause those whom they actuate, to see danger only on one side; and serve to veil and even second the arts of influence on the other. Real patriots, who may resist the intrigues of the favorite, are liable to become suspected and odious; while its tools and dupes usurp the applause and confidence of the people, to surrender their interests.

The great rule of conduct for us, in regard to foreign nations is, in extending our commercial relations, to have with them as little political connection as possible. So far as we have already formed engagements, let them be fulfilled with perfect good faith. Here let us stop.

Europe has a set of primary interests, which to us have none, or a very remote relation. Hence she must be engaged in frequent controversies, the causes of which are essentially foreign to our concerns. Hence, therefore, it must be unwise in us to implicate ourselves, by artificial ties, in the ordinary vicissitudes of her politics, or the ordinary combinations and collisions of her friendships and enmities.

Our detached and distant situation invites and enables us to pursue a different course. If we remain one people, under an efficient government, the period is not far off when we may defy material injury from external annoyance; when we may take such an attitude as will cause the neutrality we may at any time resolve upon, to be scrupulously respected; when belligerent nations, under the impossibility of making acquisitions upon us, will not lightly hazard the giving us provocation; when we may choose peace or war, as our interest, guided by justice, shall counsel.

Why forego the advantages of so peculiar a situation? Why quit our own, to stand upon foreign ground? Why, by interweaving our destiny with that of any part of Europe, entangle our peace and prosperity in the toils of European ambition, rivalship, interest, humor, or caprice?

'Tis our true policy to steer clear of permanent alliances, with any portion of the foreign world. So far, I mean, as we are now at liberty to do it, for let me not be understood as capable of patronizing infidelity to existing engagements (I hold the maxim no less applicable to public than to private affairs, that honesty is always the best policy). I repeat it, therefore, let those engagements be observed in their genuine sense. But, in my opinion, it is unnecessary and would be unwise to extend them.

Taking care always to keep ourselves, by suitable establishments, on a respectably defensive posture, we may safely trust to temporary alliances for extraordinary emergencies.

Harmony, liberal intercourse with all nations, are recommended by policy, humanity, and interest. But even our commercial policy should hold an equal and impartial hand: neither seeking nor granting exclusive favors or preferences; consulting the natural course of things; diffusing and diversifying by gentle means the streams of commerce, but forcing nothing; establishing with powers so disposed; in order to give to trade a stable course, to define the rights of our merchants, and to enable the government to support them; conventional rules of intercourse, the best that present circumstances and mutual opinion will permit, but temporary, and liable to be from time to time abandoned or varied, as experience and circumstances shall dictate; constantly keeping in view, that 'tis folly in one nation to look for disinterested favors from another; that it must pay with a portion of its independence for whatever it may accept under that character; that by such acceptance, it may place itself in the condition of having given equivalents for nominal favors and yet of being reproached with ingratitude for not giving more. There can be no greater error than to expect, or calculate upon, real favors from nation to nation. 'Tis all illusion which experience must cure, which a just pride ought to discard.

In offering to you, my countrymen, these counsels of an old and affectionate friend, I dare not hope they will make the strong and lasting impression I could wish, that they will control the usual current of the passions, or prevent our nation from running the course which has hitherto marked the destiny of nations. But if I may even flatter myself that they may be productive of some partial benefit, some occasional good; that they may now and then recur to moderate the fury of party spirit, to warn against the mischiefs of foreign intrigue, to guard against the impostures of pretended patriotism; this hope will be a full recompense for the solicitude for your welfare, by which they have been dictated.

How far, in the discharge of my official duties, I have been guided by the principles which have been delineated, the public records and other evidences of my conduct must witness to you and to the world. To myself the assurance of my own conscience is, that I have at least believed myself to be guided by them.

In relation to the still subsisting war in Europe, my proclamation of April 22, 1793, is the index of my plan. Sanctioned by your approving voice, and by that of your representatives in both houses of Congress, the spirit of that measure has continually governed me, uninfluenced by any attempts to deter or divert me from it.

After deliberate examination, with the aid of the best lights I could obtain, I was well satisfied that our country, under all the circumstances of the case, had a right to take, and was bound in duty and interest to take, a neutral position. Having taken it, I determined, as far as should depend upon me, to maintain it with moderation, perseverance, and firmness.

The considerations which respect the right to hold this conduct, it is not necessary, on this occasion, to detail. I will only observe, that, according to my understanding of the matter, that right, so far from being denied by any of the belligerent powers, has been virtually admitted by all.

The duty of holding a neutral conduct may be inferred, without anything more, from the obligation which justice and humanity impose on every nation, in cases in which it is free to act, to maintain inviolate the relations of peace and amity towards other nations.

The inducements of interest for observing that conduct will best be referred to your own reflection and experience. With me, a predominant motive has been to endeavor to gain time to our country to settle and mature its yet recent institutions, and to progress, without interruption, to that degree of strength and consistency which is necessary to give it, humanly speaking, the command of its own fortunes.

Though in reviewing the incidents of my administration, I am unconscious of intentional error, I am nevertheless too sensible of my defects not to think it probable that I may have committed many errors. Whatever they may be, I fervently beseech the Almighty to avert or mitigate the evils to which they may tend. I shall also carry with me the hope that my country will never cease to view them with indulgence, and that after forty-five years of my life dedicated to its service, with an upright zeal, the faults of incompetent abilities will be consigned to oblivion, as myself must soon be to the mansions of rest.

Relying on its kindness in this as in other things, and actuated by that fervent love towards in which is so natural to a man who views in it the native soil of himself and his progenitors for several generations, I anticipate with pleasing expectation that retreat, in which I promise myself to realize, without alloy, the sweet enjoyment of partaking, in the midst of my fellow citizens, the benign influence of good laws under a free government, the ever favorite object of my heart, and the happy reward, as I trust, of our mutual cares, labors, and dangers.

G. WASHINGTON.

—·····✳·····—

—⸳⸳⸳⸹⸳⸳⸳—

The ACKNOWLEDGMENTS

The British wit and essayist G. K. Chesterton, in his autobiography, summed up his life's goal: "The chief idea of my life . . . taking things with gratitude and not taking things for granted." This expresses my sentiments. I've tried not to take anything or anyone for granted while writing this pamphlet. Rather, I've tried to express thankful praise. And first, foremost, and always, I must acknowledge God. Without the gracious gifts bestowed upon me by my God, I could have never thought these thoughts nor written these words. He knows my heart.

John Adair is a walking, talking, one man think tank. John gave me a listening ear when I needed to try-out ideas, no matter how nutty . . . and he didn't laugh at them all—that's a true friend indeed. Thanks, John, for your insightful comments on the manuscript and for enduring my Jeterisms for all these years.

Jim Craft has the eyes of an eagle. An errant comma or semicolon is like a trout trying to hide in the shadows. Jim sees it and swoops down upon it with lightening speed, agility, and power. I'm grateful to you, Jim, for making this pamphlet more than it would have been without your talents.

Nancy Gustine is a design genius. The book you hold in your hands is attractive because she made it so. If it had been left up to me, you'd have a few loose-leaf papers with the corners bent—hardly the stuff books are made of. I assure you, if there's anything unattractive about this book it's wholly my fault, because like a darn fool I didn't listen to her when I should have. Thank you, Nancy, for your keen eye, your untiring professionalism, and your generous spirit.

Katy Merritt possesses the rarest gift of all for those of us in the writing profession—she has the keen eye of a first-class editor and a feel for words that makes her a superior writer. I suppose it's the poet in her. Without a doubt, the pamphlet you hold in your hands would have been rougher hewed without Katy's sanding and finishing touches. Editors never receive the praise or recognition they deserve, but they are the makers of books and authors. Thank you Katy for helping make me a better writer and making this pamphlet a better product.

T. Scott Stromberg was as giddy as a schoolgirl when I asked him to draw the cover for this pamphlet. He said it would give him an opportunity to work in black and white and in pencil. I don't understand why that would tickle his fancy, but I'm grateful he was happy to do it and do such unique artwork.

A man's legacy is found in his family. No writer can accomplish much without the love and support of his intimates, even if he were to win literary prizes and sell millions of copies. All things turn to dust, except love. So, to Derrick Jr., Austin, Cierra, Travis, and Trey, thank you for loving your sometimes unlovable daddy and letting me write.

Christy, my wife, is the polar star in our home. She is the one we all orbit around. Without her aid, chaos would reign. Without her brilliance, darkness would descend. Without her love, life would not be worth the living. She is my first and best reader. And like the Father above, she knows my heart.

DERRICK G. JETER
July 31, 2011
McKinney, Texas

—⸰⸰⸰※⸰⸰⸰—

The
ENDNOTES

The author and publisher have made all reasonable efforts to locate sources and obtain permissions where necessary for the quotations used in this pamphlet. In the event of unintentional omissions, the publisher will gladly incorporate modifications in future editions.

1. Thomas Jefferson to James Callender, October 6, 1799, in *The Works of Thomas Jefferson*, Federal Edition, vol. 9, ed. Paul Leicester Ford (New York: G. P. Putnam's Sons, 1905), 84–85.

2. William Stoughton, as quoted in Ronald C. White Jr., *Lincoln's Greatest Speech: The Second Inaugural* (New York: Simon & Schuster, 2002), 256.

3. Louis Brandeis, *Whitney v. California*, 274 U.S. 357 (1927), http://supreme.justia.com/us/274/357/case.html, accessed September 25, 2010.

4. George Whitefield to Samuel Haven and Samuel Langdom, 1763, as quoted in Jerome Dean Mahaffey, *Preaching Politics: The Religious Rhetoric of George Whitefield and the Founding of a New Nation* (Waco, Tex.: Baylor University Press, 2007), 190.

5. Ronald Reagan, "Encroaching Control (The Peril of Ever Expanding Government)," Chamber of Commerce, Phoenix, Arizona, March 30, 1961, in *A Time for Choosing: The Speeches of Ronald Reagan*, 1961–1982 (Chicago: Regnery Gateway, 1983), 38.

6. Ronald J. Pestritto and William J. Atto, eds., *American Progressivism: A Reader* (Lanham, Md.: Lexington Books, 2008), 3.

7. Woodrow Wilson, "What is Progress?" from *The New Freedom*, quoted in Pestritto and Atto, eds., *American Progressivism*, 50.

8. Thomas Jefferson to Jeudy de L'Hommande, August 9, 1787, in *The Papers of Thomas Jefferson Digital Edition*, ed. Barbara B. Oberg and J. Jefferson Looney (Charlottesville: University of Virginia Press, Rotunda, 2008), http://rotunda.upress.virginia.edu/founders/TSJN-01-12-02-0017, accessed April 22, 2011.

9. Thomas Jefferson to Edward Carrington, May 27, 1788, in *The Papers of Thomas Jefferson Digital Edition*, ed. Barbara B. Oberg and J. Jefferson Looney, http://rotunda.upress.virginia.edu/founders/TSJN-01-13-02-0120, accessed April 22, 2011.

10. James H. Hutson, *Religion and the Founding of the American Republic* (Washington, D.C.: Library of Congress, 1998), 81.

11. "Valerius Poplicola" (Samuel Adams), Boston Gazette, October 4, 1772, *The Writings of Samuel Adams*, ed. Harry Alonzo Cushing (New York: G. P. Putnam's Sons, 1904–1908), 2:336.

12. Alexis de Tocqueville, *Democracy in America*, 1.1.2, trans. Harvey C. Mansfield and Delba Winthrop (Chicago: The University of Chicago Press, 2000), 43–44.

13. Robert H. Bork, *Slouching Towards Gomorrah: Modern Liberalism and American Decline* (New York: Regan-Books, 1996), 8–9.

14. Michael Novak, "The Causes of Virtue," speech given in Washington, D.C., January 31, 1994, as quoted in Charles Colson and Nancy Pearcey, *How Now Shall We Live?* (Wheaton, Ill.: Tyndale House, 1999), 377 (emphasis in original).

15. Aleksandr Solzhenitsyn, "Templeton Lecture," May 10, 1983, trans. Alexis Klimoff, in *The Solzhenitsyn Reader: New and Essential Writings, 1947–2005*, ed. Edward E. Ericson Jr. and Daniel J. Mahoney (Wilmington, Del.: ISI Books, 2006), 577.

16. Abraham Lincoln, "Proclamation Appointing a National Fast Day," March 30, 1863, in *The Collected Works of Abraham Lincoln*, vol. 6, ed. Roy P. Basler (New Brunswick, N.J.: Rutgers University Press, 1953), 155–56.

17. Thomas Jefferson, *Notes on the State of Virginia*, in *Thomas Jefferson: Writings* (New York: The Library of America, 1984), 289.

18. Georg Wilhelm Friedrich Hegel, *Philosophy of History*, trans. J. Sibree (New York: American Home Library, 1902), 87.

19. Hegel, *Philosophy of Rights*, trans. S. W. Dyde (London: George Bell and Sons, 1896), 247, 276.

20. Solzhenitsyn, "Templeton Lecture," trans. Alexis Klimoff, in *The Solzhenitsyn Reader*, 579.

21. Tocqueville, *Democracy in America*, 1.1.2, trans. Harvey C. Mansfield and Delba Winthrop, 42.

22. Tocqueville, *Democracy in America*, 1.1.2, trans. Harvey C. Mansfield and Delba Winthrop, 42.

23. Samuel Adams, as quoted in Ira Stoll, *Samuel Adams: A Life* (New York: Free Press, 2008), 25.

24. John Adams, "To the Officers of the First Brigade of the Third Division of the Militia of Massachusetts," October 11, 1798, *The Works of John Adams, Second President of the United States*, ed. Charles Francis Adams (Boston: Little, Brown and Company, 1854), 9:229.

25. Tocqueville, *Democracy in America*, 2.4.6, trans. Harvey C. Mansfield and Delba Winthrop, 663.

26. Edward Gibbon, *The Decline and Fall of the Roman Empire*, vol. 1 (New York: The Heritage Press, 1946), 464 (emphasis mine).

27. Karl Marx and Frederick Engels, *The Communist Manifesto: A Modern Edition* (London: Verso, 1998), 60.

28. Marx and Engels, *The Communist Manifesto*, 60–61.

29. Chuck Colson, *The Enduring Revolution: The Battle to Change the Human Heart* (Uhrichsville, Ohio: Barbour & Co., 1996), 47.

30. Vigen Guroian, *Rallying the Really Human Things: The Moral Imagination in Politics, Literature, and Everyday Life* (Wilmington, Del.: ISI Books, 2005), 191.

31. *Amistad*, Steven Spielberg, director, DVD (1997; Universal City, Cal.: DreamWorks, 1999).

32. Walt Whitman, *Leaves of Grass* (New York: Barnes & Noble, 1997), 5.

33. Tocqueville, *Democracy in America*, 1.2.9, trans. Harvey C. Mansfield and Delba Winthrop, 282.

34. Thomas Paine, *Common Sense*, in *Thomas Paine: Collected Works* (New York: The Library of America, 1995), 43.

35. Quoted from the handwritten history of Rev. Ethan Allen, "Washington Parish, Washington City" in the Library of Congress MMC Collection, 1167, MSS, as quoted in James H. Hutson, *Religion and the Founding of the American Republic*, 96.

36. Gordon S. Wood, *Revolutionary Characters: What Made the Founders Different?* (New York: Penguin Press, 2006), front flap.

37. Theodore Roosevelt, as quoted in Edward J. Renehan Jr., *The Lion's Pride: Theodore Roosevelt and His Family in Peace and War* (New York: Oxford University Press, 1998), 72.

38. Max Farrand, ed., The Records of the Federal Constitution of 1787 [Farrando's Records] (New Haven, Conn.: Yale University Press, 1911), 3:85, sec. 116, http://memory.loc.gov/ll/llfr/003/0000/00890085.tif, accessed February 2, 2011.

39. Adrian Goldsworthy, *How Rome Fell: Death of a Superpower* (New Haven, Conn.: Yale University Press, 2009), 415.

40. E. B. White, "Intimation," in One Man's Meat (Gardiner, Maine: Tilbury House, 1997), 221.

41. Marc D. Guerra, *Christians as Political Animals: Taking the Measure of Modernity and Modern Democracy* (Wilmington, Del.: ISI Books, 2010), 85.

42. John Adams to Zabdiel Adams, June 21, 1776, http://www.masshist.org/publications/apde/portia.php?id=AFC02d011, accessed July 30, 2011.

43. Daniel Webster, "Compromise Bill," Speech before the United States Senate, Washington, D.C., July 17, 1850.

44. George Mason to Patrick Henry, as quoted in George Morgan, *The True Patrick Henry* (Philadelphia: J. B. Lippincott, 1907), 311.

45. John Adams to Abigail Adams, Philadelphia, Pennsylvania, July 7, 1775, in *My Dearest Friend: Letters of Abigail and John Adams*, eds. Margaret A. Hogan and C. James Taylor (Cambridge, Mass.: The Belknap Press of Harvard University Press, 2007), 69.

—·········—

ABOUT *the* AUTHOR

DERRICK G. JETER speaks and writes on the vital topics of faith and freedom. Derrick believes, as did America's Founding Fathers, that only a religious and virtuous people are capable of winning, securing, and maintaining liberty. America's brave forefathers won liberty with arms and blood. They secured liberty with pen and ink. We will maintain liberty with vigilance to the principles they laid down in the Declaration of Independence, the Constitution, and the Bill of Rights. Our task today is no less important than theirs in the eighteenth century, nor is it for the faint of heart. Only the courageous can maintain liberty—just as only the courageous can win and secure liberty. If we mean to live free, we must be brave.

For more information about publications by Derrick or to book a speaking engagement, please contact him by visiting his website at www.derrickjeter.com, emailing him at derrick@derrickjeter.com, or becoming a follower on Twitter at www.twitter.com/derrickjeter.

—••••✼••••—

ABOUT *the* ARTIST *and* COVER

T. SCOTT STROMBERG is an illustrator, designer, and fine artist who resides in Frisco, Texas, with his beautiful wife and two sons. If you would like to view more of his work, you can visit his website at www.tscottstromberg.com or follow his blog at www.addmorenoise.com. For their constant support and prayers, T. Scott would like to thank his wife Sammie, his sons, and all those friends and family who have supported his creative endeavors throughout his life. *Soli Deo Gloria.*

The *O America!* cover is a pen and ink illustration made to mimic classic linoleum prints. The subject matter was inspired by the content of this pamphlet and depicts a frustrated Uncle Sam contemplating the state of liberty in America today. Prints of the illustration can be obtained by contacting T. Scott at his website: www.tscottstromberg.com.

—····✕····—

ABOUT *the* PAMPHLET

PAMPHLETS in our country's history were popular and effective means of educating and motivating the American people to action on issues crucial to the nation, especially in the eighteenth and nineteenth centuries. The most famous of these early pamphleteers and pamphlets was Thomas Paine and his *Common Sense*. So important was the publication of pamphlets in early America that Thomas Jefferson, writing to James Callender in 1799, said, "[Pamphlets] inform the thinking part of the nation . . . [and] set the people to rights."

In keeping with the spirit of setting the people to rights, each JETER PRESS pamphlet seeks, in a thoughtful and historical fashion, to educate citizens on critical questions facing America in the twenty-first century and to persuade them that practical and civil action is not only necessary but required if America is to remain a free and prosperous nation.

—⁓⁓✲⁓⁓—

ABOUT *the* PUBLISHER

THE JETER PRESS is a small, independent publishing house established in 2011 in the Dallas area.

Our vision is to produce quality fiction and nonfiction print books, eBooks, and audio books that grapple with the important questions of faith and freedom. We strive to publish works that are engaging to the mind, appealing to the eye, and enriching to the spirit. We believe the surest way to fulfill this vision is to publish writing that is crisp and thoughtful, not preachy; to tell stories that are historical and literary, not lecture-like; and to present publications that are redemptive and attractive, not ugly. In this way, books from THE JETER PRESS garner wisdom from the past and project hope for the future, so our readers might be emboldened to live courageous and free lives in the present.

—···❋···—

FOR *the* GLORY *of* GOD
and the GOOD *of the* PEOPLE

—···❋···—

BE BRAVE LIVE FREE

www.ingramcontent.com/pod-product-compliance
Lightning Source LLC
Chambersburg PA
CBHW060936040426
42445CB00011B/892